BUILD A **SAFER WORLD**
THROUGH
CONCEALED CARRY
& **SELF-DEFENSE**

BY
NICK DAHLBERG
WITH
TOM DAHLBERG & CHRIS SCHUTROP
EDITED BY **RICK CARLILE**
PHOTOS BY **JOSHUA FLOM**

Carlile Originals

Carrying a Gun
Build A Safer World Through Concealed Carry & Self-Defense

By Nick Dahlberg, Chris Schutrop and Tom Dahlberg

Edited and illustrated by Rick Carlile
Photographs by Joshua Flom (except where separately credited). "About the Authors" photos courtesy Midwest Carry Academy. "The Smith & Wesson Bodyguard 380 Pistol" photo by Avicennasis, used under CC BY-SA 3.0 license (see creativecommons.org/licenses/by-sa/3.0/).

First edition published 2019

Published in the United States of America

ISBN-13: 978-1-949117-03-5
ISBN-10: 1949117030

THE **ACTION** PUBLISHERS

WWW.CARLILE.MEDIA

ABOUT THE AUTHORS

Chris Schutrop is the CEO of Midwest Carry Academy (MCA) and National Carry Academy (NCA), innovative online and in-person gun training enterprises which have helped thousands of gun owners attain their concealed carry permits and learn how to defend themselves effectively with an assortment of firearms. MCA and NCA have transformed the process of acquiring the permit to carry by making information and training more accessible, more effective, and inexpensive, teaching 30,000 students per year in 27 states. Chris is also a founder of Stock and Barrel Gun Club. Stock and Barrel operates a luxury gun range in both Chanhassen and Eagan, Minnesota. S&B provides its members and walk-ins with the premier indoor shooting experience in the Midwest driven by a vision that makes the firing range and gun store friendly, safe, and educational for everyone from the very young to the very old, male and female, novices to competitive shooters, and also for industry experts and law enforcement professionals. It offers an array of membership options including a Caliber Club level, with access to a luxurious private shooting range and clubhouse.

Nick Dahlberg is a co-founder of Midwest Carry Academy, National Carry Academy, and the Stock and Barrel Gun Club. As operations manager he specializes in firearms training programs. Nick is a top-ranked competitive shooter and NRA-certified trainer. He is the lead instructor of the MCA, NCA, and Stock and Barrel self-defense curriculum. Having acquired his own knowledge and skills under and alongside Special Forces instructors, he has trained every level of shooter from neophyte to law enforcement specialist, gaining recognition as a welcoming, engaging, and effective coach and mentor. Nick created the Safety Operations Procedures and protocols for MCA, NCA, and Stock and Barrel, while overseeing the layouts and techniques for building and sustaining a safe and attractive indoor gun range. He has spent years developing the concealed carry permit and advanced gun training content used in all of the course work at MCA, NCA and Stock and Barrel.

Tom Dahlberg is a firearms enthusiast, recreational shooter, hunter, and freelance writer. He has had his concealed carry permit for fifteen years, relying on the training he has received from MCA and the Stock and Barrel Gun Club where he is an active Caliber Club member. He credits the instruction he has received under Nick and Chris with taking him from a complete novice to a new competitive shooter.

Nick Dahlberg

The Stock & Barrel Gun Club.

TABLE OF CONTENTS

PART 1

THE PHILOSOPHY OF SELF-DEFENSE

CHAPTER 1

IS SELF-DEFENSE REALLY A RIGHT?

If you do not know why your right to self-defense is really a right, it will undermine your confidence. Philosophical clarity is the most important aspect of your readiness and confidence in the face of a threat. If you cannot defend yourself with *conviction*, you may make things worse than they would be if you threw yourself on the mercy of the aggressor.

If you cannot be sure of the morality of self-defense, you may as well forget the whole idea of defending yourself with deadly force. You will not do so effectively. You will make a mess of it, perhaps injuring yourself or another in a fashion which will prove you never should have tried in the first place. You cannot defend yourself effectively and responsibly without confidence. You have to be decisive. You cannot possibly be confident and decisive without a firm belief in the right and responsibility to defend yourself.

"Nothing could be more natural than fighting for one's life."

Moral doubt, as the most fundamental form of self-doubt, is the most comprehensive attack on your confidence, making all other preparation pointless. Self-defense starts with a confident conviction that you have the right to fight and even kill someone else whenever and wherever they are threatening you with injury or death.

Of course, most people believe that they, and everyone else, have a 'right' to self-defense. This is often anchored in the notion that nothing could be more natural than fighting for one's life. In the wild, we can see that self-defense is overwhelmingly natural, not that it is consistently successful. Death removes our opportunity to be what we are by nature, to exercise *the rest* of our nature.

To put it another way, our life is our natural property, and no one has the right to take it away from us unless we have taken it away from someone else without cause. The right to our property, our lives, is reflected in our duty to respect the lives, the property, of others. This, of course, is an entirely different account of our right to life than any purely natural account.

When we begin to think carefully about it, we soon realize that our right to self-defense is not revealed, not rationally justified, by nature alone. Animals have a survival instinct but no related duties. We do not take predators out of the wild and put them on trial for murder. They do not have a duty to preserve the lives of other animals. In that case they do not have a right to their own life. Animals live in a moral and material ecosystem where every rational human being admits that justice is in the interest of the stronger. Human moral categories do not apply. If animals do not have duties, they do not have rights. Predation is not a right, and the prey does not have the duty to submit. It is all just a power struggle without moral questions. Animals, we usually agree, are designed this way.

By contrast, most of us believe that human beings are *not* designed this way. Our traditional belief in the right to life is an assertion of a whole world-view in which man *transcends nature.* In both the human or animal arena self-defense is natural, predictable, consistent with natural law. In the meantime nature alone does not announce anyone's *right* to kill, even when it gives them the opportunity and the power to do so. It is just a brute fact. If we take the position that nature makes the right of the stronger clear, then the government, being stronger, will not hesitate to eliminate the right to life. This punishment is popular when someone, a murderer, has adopted exactly the same position and acted on it. But in this case we have rejected the idea that the human and animal arenas are different, that human beings are supposed to be more than natural, that they are supposed to be just. Justice must be a notion that transcends nature.

"Justice must be a notion that transcends nature."

And so the fly in the ointment of the notion that self-defense is anchored in natural law alone is that there are plenty of people who are willing to argue that murder, or abuse, is just as natural. If naturality is the standard of a right, then there might be the right to commit what we normally categorize as crimes. It is perfectly natural for people to misbehave. Although this does not lead to the conclusion that self-defense is not a natural right, it leads to the question "How, on a purely natural basis, could we know what a right is? Aggression seems to be just as natural as self-defense." A philosopher once said "As a result of studying nature alone one is as likely to become a headhunter as a liberal."

Yet, in spite of our doubt that nature speaks for itself when it comes to morality and rights, the social contract, generally speaking, is supposed to be arranged to fulfill our nature, not suppress or destroy it. And this is exactly why arguments about what is natural for human beings has always been and always will be the philosophical heart and soul of politics. The proponent of natural rights asks us "What could be more natural than our right to save our own lives in the light of unjustified aggression?" Natural rights depend upon our agreement about what is natural and agreement that that which is natural, at least for the most part, *is good.* It is both natural to fight for our lives and to attack each other as nothing more than a will to power. Both central tendencies are natural. Only one is good. We are moving past nature when we reach for agreement about what 'justifies' the kind of aggression which could result in someone else's death, besides self-defense. The good and the just transcend what we can learn from nature.

Nothing guarantees agreement about what is natural or even that what is natural is good. One of the ironies, or inconsistencies, in the left's traditional attack on the right of self-defense is that it is actually anchored in the implicit notion that what is natural is not necessarily what is good. In the meantime the left also fancies itself the champion of what is natural as if *everything* that is natural is good.

"We are sovereign individuals limited only by the sovereignty of other individuals."

In any event, we give the left an opening when we argue that the right to life, to self-defense, has a purely natural foundation. In that case, the left can simply start agreeing with most of us that what is natural is not necessarily what is good.

The religious concept of human rights is actually more consistent and clear than the notion of natural human rights. And this is why most of us are in agreement that the freedom we find in the American tradition, including the right to self-defense, is not actually anchored in any kind of naturalism but, rather, the Judeo-Christian world-view.

In the first place, the notion that self-defense is a God-given right is not at all inconsistent with the notion that self-defense is entirely natural. In effect, self-defense as a God-given right is anchored in the proposition that God designed us this way, and it is normative, good, because God intended it. Nature may not be an authority about what is good, but God is. We are not just natural, we are made in the image of God, and are therefore, like God, sovereign individuals *limited only by the sovereignty of other individuals.* This tradition more clearly and consistently implies that self-defense is a sovereign right while murder clearly is not. Murder, no matter how natural, is an attack on the sovereignty given to individuals by God. Nature can only make a tyrant sovereign by *force*, not by right.

Clearly, the perpetual battle between left and right is simply a battle between secularists who think we should look only to nature (as diverse and relative as expert views of nature are) and those who insist that we look to our western religious revelation and tradition. It is God who declared that His creation is good, that man is made in His image, and that therefore both man and nature are to be nurtured and protected by stewards, including governments. We doubt that the libertarians, who look only to nature, can defend our right to self-defense as well, as coherently, as Christian traditionalists.

"To exercise the rights is to assert the tradition. To assert the tradition is to preserve the tradition."

But just as not everyone sees Nature the same way, arguing that it is as natural to kill others as it is to defend oneself, not everyone has the same theology, or any theology at all. The notion of God-given rights may be revealed in history, it may be a fact, captured in the Ten Commandments (thou shalt not murder) but those of us who believe it cannot force others to do so.

And so the right to self-defense must be regarded as a *tradition*, which is absolutely, metaphysically correct in the eyes of God. Just because this is a tradition does not imply that it is not absolutely true. But it does in imply this practical principle.

Sustaining the tradition of self-defense requires the vigorous exercise of the rights which the *tradition* identifies. To exercise the rights is to assert the tradition. To assert the tradition is to preserve the tradition.

The right of self-defense cannot be separated from a particular way of looking at the world and its human beings. If you believe that self-defense is a right, if you share the traditional basis of this, then you have a duty to yourself and everyone who stands with you to exercise it, otherwise it will disappear precisely because there is no way to force the opponents of self-defense to admit that there is either a God-given basis for the right or a natural basis. Any proposed right is not so overwhelmingly natural that a naturalistic culture will not end up eliminating it. The right is granted by the tradition, and the tradition becomes irrelevant when people do not act on it, when they fail to engage in its rituals. And so we conclude that keeping and bearing arms is more than just a hobby, it is a precious ritual which asserts a precious tradition.

Many people implicitly know that keeping and bearing arms is a ritual and are accused by the left of making guns a 'life-style.' These accusers cannot understand what is happening. Subconsciously many Americans understand the connection between gun ownership and the preservation of the whole tradition, the whole world-view. Their behavior seems ritualistic and it is quite rightly ritualistic. The left then accuses the traditionalists of turning their gun ownership into a sacrament. But this is not what is happening. What is happening is that people approach their right to keep and bear arms as more than a hobby, more than entertainment, more than hunting – and they must. *It is essential to the whole tradition which raises man above nature and asserts his right to live and defend himself.* It is all about the value of human life. Gun ownership is not a sacrament, but of necessity it is a traditional ritual which needs to be engaged in with widespread regularity. Organizations like the NRA understand this implicitly. The objective is not simply to protect our rights in the abstract, but to promote the exercise of them ritualistically, with regularity, as the most powerful way in which we assert the tradition over and over again. The NRA has good reason, as do we, to promote gun ownership *as a life-style*, the very thing which the left cannot understand in its naiveté about how rights, as traditional artifacts, are proposed and preserved.

"If you lose your right to intimidate criminals, including criminal governments, you will soon find that you have lost everything else you believe in."

By exercising your right to self-defense, you train and condition society to accept and even embrace the tradition. This is a democratic and traditional process and victory. If you do not participate, while believing in the tradition, you have failed to understand how we sustain such a tradition, how fragile the dominance of the tradition becomes when it is not asserted daily and en masse. And remember, *practically* speaking, we are talking about the most important dimension of the tradition. If you lose your right to intimidate criminals, including criminal governments, you will soon find that you have lost everything else you believe in. Why is gun ownership and self-defense a right? Because the loss of this *life-style*, this tradition, results in the loss of the other values established by the tradition – the right to free speech, the right to property, liberty, the pursuit of happiness, all of which require survival and just government. When one of our rights is violated, they are all violated. The whole tradition which argues that we have rights as human beings, is violated, rejected, by the suppression of one right.

If only a small minority explicitly exercise their right to self-defense, too many voters, and too many politicians, will conclude that traditional or not, the 'right' is not important enough, to enough people, to worry about. We must make it an overwhelmingly democratic and true perception that self-defense is an inviolable right (because we believe it really is) and that any government that would take it away from us, is an illegitimate government.

It is important to remember, that even from a purely naturalistic point of view, those who cannot kill, will inevitably be subjugated and abused by those who can. Every tyrant, every criminal, exploits the incapacity and/or unwillingness of a people to engage in self-defense.

And so we come to the more practical question of whether or not you can exercise your right to self-defense, in a meaningful way, without the great equalizer – the gun. The practical answer to this practical question is "No, you can't."

The gun is quite literally the practical fulfillment of the God-given right to self-defense.

Without the gun, the right to self-defense is practically meaningless, and this may be precisely why this right was not vigorously asserted and defended, especially by government itself, until the gun was invented. It was a real right, but could not be applied practically speaking.

Without the gun women, even children, and average men, cannot make their right to self-defense a real threat to those who would harm them, subjugate them, murder them. This leads us to the next very dramatic conclusion.

The gun is quite literally the fulfillment of democracy.

The gun democratizes power. It gives even the common man as much power, in principle, as criminal experts who could otherwise overwhelm him with a sword, with fists, with a gang. It also gives the common man as much power as the police, who would otherwise be in a position to impose a police state. Finally, in principle, the gun gives the people at large as much power as the military, assuming that any military subjugation of the people would be self-defeating if it required the extermination of the people using weapons of mass destruction. We reject the notion that a militia cannot defeat a standing army. We once thought that the Viet Cong and the vastly inferior North Vietnamese army could not defeat an army with weapons of mass destruction, but they did. Our forefathers beat the most powerful, professional army on earth at that time, with a non-professional force often using inferior arms.

Given the western religious tradition, we do not assert the right to take someone else's life but, instead, the right to defend our own and that of others. We escape from any naturalistic confusion in which naturalness becomes the standard of a right. Instead our religious tradition coherently suggests that we have the right to defend our lives against those naturalists who think it is perfectly natural to take our substance and/or kill us. Every tyrant, every criminal is a naturalist. They believe that justice is whatever satisfies the stronger. Those of us who believe in civilization cannot afford to be naturalists.

> **"In defending yourself you are defending the whole community."**

Finally, it is worth noticing that self-defense is not part of some caricature of rugged individualism. In defending yourself you are defending the whole community. Remember, keeping and bearing arms *is* a ritual which asserts a whole tradition, a whole life-style, a form of life. You secure your neighbor by coming directly to his aid and by helping to sustain a tradition of self-defense which makes it very risky for criminals to assume that your neighbor is unarmed and incapacitated. Just as your vote may protect your neighbor's freedom and security, your gun, and your ability to use it as an expression of a national tradition, secures your neighbors right to life, property, and liberty.

The weak are always safer, more secure in their rights, when living among the strong and the just.

CHAPTER 2

WHOSE RESPONSIBILITY IS YOUR DEFENSE?

One strategy the left uses to take away the right of self-defense is to reduce it to the right to be defended by the government. This is a clever rhetorical strategy because it suggests the government must be given all of the power required to do so. Our right is the government's duty, and a massive amount of power is needed to perform this duty including constant surveillance.

This transfer of responsibility from us to the government is also clever because you *do* have the right to be defended by the government. The government has been set up to protect your rights, including your right to life and private property.

But it does not follow that you have given up your right to self-defense when you remind the government that it is supposed to secure your life and property. It cannot do so by restricting your gun rights.

"The primary manner in which the government protects us is with after-the-fact prosecution, not the ready defense of our persons."

We have established government, primarily the justice system, to secure our freedom and our property. But unfortunately, the government, without completely controlling us and our property, does not actually have the wherewithal to protect us on a day to day basis. The primary manner in which it protects us is with after-the-fact prosecution, not the ready defense of our persons. If being our body guard is the government's responsibility, it is one that cannot be lived up to. If the only right we have is the right to the government's bodily protection, then the right becomes almost meaningless.

Most people, even some people on the left, stipulate to this obvious reality. But they will argue that if we have a private right to self-defense, then we have coopted the proper function of government. This is especially true if we start organizing into mutual defense relationships, like neighborhood or state militias.

"When the people are disarmed the government can <u>use</u> the criminals."

It is tempting to respond by taking the position that our personal defense is not, in fact, a proper role of government. This would result in a simple, clear, unmistakable division of labor which would force citizens as such to get serious about their own self-defense. And for all we know, if our defense, or all of the police functions, were handed over to the people, we would be better off. There is no space to deal with this here except to say that this vision is less radical than you might suppose. Imagine that there were still elected sheriffs and their deputies, *including most of us*, but no so-called professional police departments. The whole idea of professional, unelected police, might be undemocratic. We can debate this interesting question elsewhere.

In any event, the government cannot protect each individual and therefore *we should not make this an explicit duty of the government.* In point of fact, we cannot sue the police for not being there when they are really needed.

For the most part, the government cannot protect you. We might simply say that the government never has and never will be able to protect you from nature. The full meaning of this is to be found in hurricane Katrina and its aftermath. It is perfectly natural for both the civilian and government criminals to disarm and subjugate you given a return to a state of nature induced by such a natural disaster. *You* are finally responsible for your own self-defense, for the assertion of our tradition over and against nature, or there will always be nothing but a state of nature where one highly successful gang calls itself the government.

If you deny your responsibility, the government will abandon any recognition of the tradition of self-defense, and it will subjugate you either directly, or by failing to control the criminals. When the people are disarmed the government can *use* the criminals. Do as the government says and it will try to protect you. Otherwise you are on your own without even the right, let alone the tools, to defend yourself. This kind of politics is part of the natural disposition of power. First the government removes your right and your practical capacity to defend yourself. Then it trades its meager protection for total compliance. This all starts to fall apart when the people begin to realize that the government cannot fulfill its part of the bargain.

If and when the vast majority of Americans take explicit, personal responsibility, for their private self-defense, we might find ourselves in little need of professional police departments which will morph into subsidiaries of elected sheriffs. This would be the result of something more important – a tradition of self-defense being taken for granted by both the people and the government, and a drastic reduction in violent crime.

As violent crime disappears in a society of people who are committed to defending themselves, the left will always begin to argue that self-defense has become unnecessary and then the political and cultural war over self-defense begins all over again. The left knows very well that our peace and security is a function of this commitment to self-defense. But it will always ignore this causal relationship in order to increase the power of the government. Only your commitment to *exercising* your right to self-defense, to making it a traditional ritual, even a life-style – always accepting your responsibility for your own defense – can prevent the police state that the left is always looking for.

CHAPTER 3

IS DEFENDING SOMEONE ELSE A DUTY?

If you have a right to defend yourself, then others have a duty to let you do so. They have a duty to ensure that you *may* defend yourself and *can* defend yourself in principle.

But this is *your* duty as well. Since you have the right, you also have the duty to make sure that others can exercise their right. And when you find that someone does not have the wherewithal to defend themselves, it is your duty to make sure that this is their *choice*, that they are not being constrained by the government or anyone else.

The duty concomitant to any right is the duty to make sure the right can be exercised by those who choose to do so. It is not a duty to exercise the right for them. It is not your obligation to buy a gun for your neighbor. Your duty is to make sure that *he* can buy a gun to realize his right to self-defense, to make it meaningful, practicable.

> **"It is the duty of every taxpayer to ensure a family's right to self-defense."**

But what if your neighbor wants a gun but cannot afford one? If his right to self-defense is your duty to make it possible, practicable, should the government prosecute you for not buying him a gun?

Well, in the first place, it's clear that the government should not prosecute you for in fact giving him a gun, or at least lending him a gun. It is an obvious legal theory that making firearms available to law-abiding citizens is consistent with your duty to make sure they can exercise their right to self-defense. But because this obligation is everyone's obligation, not just yours, the proper way to perform this duty which we all have (to make sure our neighbor can exercise his right) is for the government to use our tax dollars to ensure this happens. It is the duty of every taxpayer to ensure a family's right to self-defense. It follows logically, in a fashion which will make the left's collective head explode, that the government should be subsidizing the cost of gun ownership for those who cannot afford it. Just as we might argue that the right to life implies certain operations of the welfare state, the right to life and to self-defense implies that the most important welfare we can provide to law-abiding citizens is the equal opportunity to effectively defend themselves. We have vacated the rights of law-abiding people in bad neighborhoods, and good neighborhoods, when the government fails to make sure that we can all defend ourselves.

This becomes an especially interesting argument when we stop to consider the coherent principle that we do not have a duty to defend the other at the cost of our own life. The duty is to make sure that the other can defend himself. If I do not have a duty to get in between other people and their assailants, then it is all the more important to make sure that they can defend themselves if they so choose.

"No state is suggesting that our right to defend ourselves is a duty to defend the other in person. This kind of defense is grace, not a duty."

We do not know of any law which would require a concealed carry permit holder to get in between an assailant and his unprepared, unarmed victim. This would be consistent with both our rights and our duties. No state is suggesting that our right to defend ourselves is a duty to defend the other in person. This kind of defense is grace, not a duty. The other has the right to be prepared and defend himself, and we have done our duty when we ensure this politically. People are not *required* to exercise their right, and therefore we are not required to exercise it for them. We know of no 'good Samaritan' law which would require you to defend someone from an attacker even if it requires you to help afterward. Mostly such laws ensure that you cannot be sued for trying to help – but not as a warrior, as a nurse.

In effect, state law typically supports the legitimacy of a private citizen protecting another private citizen from threats to the latter's life and property. This is not a crime in itself. But it is reviewed in the same way any act of self-defense is reviewed for any violation of the statutory constraints on self-defense. (Once the threat is eliminated, everything should stop.)

Our conclusion is that there must be a distinction between moral (and religious) duties and political duties. We have a *moral* duty to protect those who cannot protect themselves. We do this for our wives and children and see no reason not to extend the favor to our neighbors. We have both a *moral and political* duty to ensure that our neighbor can exercise the universal right to self-defense. But we do not have a political, legal duty to actually stand between our neighbor and his assailant. His right to self-defense is not a right to our action on his behalf.

"The most fundamental form of welfare, based on human rights, would be the subsidy of gun ownership."

It follows from this that you must carefully consider if and when you are going to exercise your moral duty to defend those who cannot defend themselves. The law allows you to do this. God may obligate you to do this. But it is not a duty implied by the right of others to defend themselves. In the meantime, it might actually be our political duty, working through the government, to ensure that those who wish to defend themselves can do so. We do not know how to avoid the conclusion that the most fundamental form of welfare, based on human rights, would be the subsidy of gun ownership by law-abiding citizens who cannot otherwise afford it.

Ironically, the duty associated with the right to self-defense is not only an argument against gun control, but suggests that the government has the duty to proactively ensure that any law-abiding citizen who chooses to exercise his right can do so, even to the extent of making sure that he is armed, making the right meaningful. Outside of military regulation, no one has the duty to *directly* intervene for anyone else even though it may be immoral not to do so. And so it becomes all the more important to perform our actual duty – making sure that all other citizens at least have the freedom and wherewithal to defend themselves as the practical implementation of the right.

CHAPTER 4

THE POLITICS OF SELF-DEFENSE

The *philosophy* of self-defense which we have outlined here has clear implications for the *politics* of self-defense. We have established the doctrine that it is our duty to ensure the ability of others to defend themselves, by way of making the right meaningful, practicable. This means that guns need to be available and even affordable. This is a universal political duty, not just a private moral or religious duty. It is the obligation of the government to recognize and support the right to self-defense, even to the point of helping citizens acquire the means of self-defense if necessary.

This form of welfare is consistent with the government's modern insistence that the *right to life* requires laws which compel hospital emergency rooms to provide aid whether or not the patient can afford it. But wait, there's more. The modern liberal is also committed to an entire welfare state anchored in the right to life. This specific jump is no doubt controversial, while it should not be controversial that *if* the state must secure the right to life with a whole menu of welfare this should include the capacity for self-defense. If we can only realize the collective duty implied by the individual's right to life, by providing subsistence, then the state should do what it takes to make sure that everyone who wants to defend himself has a bare minimum capacity (a kind of subsistence capacity) to do so.

"The case for an armed citizenry, assured by the government itself, is extremely strong when self-defense is considered a human right."

Since the Second Amendment is also and perhaps even more fundamentally about the right to discipline or destroy a tyrannical government, there may be more than a minimum level of obligation. It is probably the duty of the government to arm the whole militia, the military competitor to any standing army and a clear limiter of its power. But in this book we are focusing only on the right to self-defense.

The case for an armed citizenry, assured by the government itself, is extremely strong when self-defense is considered a human right. Almost everyone, except some governments, says it *is* a human right.

The Second Amendment says that self-defense is an individual human right (whereas the right to intimidate the government as a militia is a collective right). The right of the individual to keep and bear arms is not to be infringed.

In the meantime, we have argued above, that the only thing which actually establishes a right, including the right to self-defense, is not nature, but our Western tradition. The political right and the obligation of the government is traditional, not naturalistic, and therefore the most important political project for proponents of our right to self-defense is to preserve and promote the tradition. We are not approaching the politics of self-defense realistically, practically, if we do not understand that without the First Amendment – our right to promote the tradition – the Second Amendment has no cultural foundation. And

"Politics is just an extension of culture."

The conclusion is that the most important aspect of the political defense of gun rights, of the right to self-defense, is the defense of the tradition which declares this right. We cannot afford to be naïve libertarians who think that nature alone and universal reason will establish and preserve this right. There is no such thing as Universal Reason and Nature is not that clear. It is subject to too much interpretation.

What we observe culturally and politically is natural, logical. Those who are working for the preservation of our right to self-defense are on average the very same people who are working to make sure that the government cannot continue to suppress the western tradition it was originally based on. They are strong proponents of the First Amendment.

In the meantime the rhetorical strategy of those who would eliminate the right to self-defense, is always based on the notion that keeping and bearing arms is ridiculous as the expression of a whole tradition. There is little need to respond to this. Most people, even on the left, know this is not true. When citizens insist on keeping and bearing arms they are clearly asserting a whole view of their rights, the nature and destiny of man, the nature of government, the fallenness of the world. To be armed is to endorse self-defense. To endorse self-

> ***"We must work to maximize the number of citizens who are exercising their God-given right to keep and bear arms memorialized in the US Constitution."***

defense is to appeal to a whole view of natural, moral, and political reality.

The left cannot win by ridiculing our commitment to the explicit ritual of keeping and bearing arms as the assertion of an entire tradition about the true nature of our human predicament (one in which self-defense from criminals, including governments, is practically necessary). When we get the left to disrespect the whole tradition, they lose and we win. This tradition is realism, and wherever and whenever people are liberated from programming, from ideology, from indoctrination in places like the government schools, they recognize this Reality. Keeping and bearing arms is not for snowflakes.

In Chapter 1 we already noticed that the right to self-defense must be asserted by exercising it. This is called 'education' and education is preservation. Education is the primary means by which we create and transfer culture.

Our political strategy is clear and simple. We must work to maximize the number of citizens who are exercising their God-given right to keep and bear arms memorialized in the US Constitution. We must not become the kind of 'experts' who patronize citizens who have the *right* to keep and bear arms. They have the right whether or not they have been trained, whether or not they are experts. Training should be used as the primary method of recruiting people into the program of exercising their right while ensuring their safety and effectiveness.

In the meantime we must exploit the modern commitment to the right to life, inherent in the welfare state, pointing out that the most fundamental form of welfare, in recognition of this right, is to arm those who cannot arm themselves. The left has worked very hard to deny guns to the people who need them the most – the law-abiding people living in the crime-ridden neighborhoods of the modern anti-utopia.

PART 2

THE PSYCHOLOGY OF SELF-DEFENSE

CHAPTER 1

BEFORE THE THREAT

First of all, denial can kill you.

The insistence by the left that you do not need to be prepared to deal with our dangerous world can ruin your life. School and theatre shootings have an extremely poignant way of illustrating this tragic truth. The left knows the world is a dangerous place just like you. But it cannot promote this simple truth and also achieve its goal of disarming private citizens. It condescends to the purported paranoia of people who carry guns and then inconsistently emphasizes how dangerous the world has become in contexts where the only proposed solution is gun control.

The rest of us do not deny that people are getting killed in churches, homes, offices, and movie theatres by criminals who cannot be stopped by gun control. We do not deny that our society has become more and more dangerous because of the chaotic moral effects of left-wing ideology. These effects cross demographic and geographic borders. We are getting

"The left refuses to accept the well-documented fact that when law-abiding citizens bear arms it reduces the crime rate."

attacked both inside and outside of the city limits.

The problem is admittedly exacerbated in the inner cities because they so often persecute and prosecute gun ownership by law-abiding citizens. In the meantime cities (see Chicago) encourage illegal gun possession by the criminal class for lack of the will and capacity to prosecute it. The left is making the world more dangerous than it needs to be in order to further its agenda. It is itself the root cause of our claims, our need to be armed. Some people, in some neighborhoods, need guns more than others. And these are precisely the people that the left wants to disarm on the ironic grounds that there is so much crime in their neighborhoods. The left refuses to accept the well-documented fact that when law-abiding citizens bear arms it reduces the crime rate.

A victim is usually attacked while unprepared due to not expecting it. The lesson is clear. It is smart, rather than paranoid, to expect it. We read in Breitbart News (January 20, 2018) about stand-up comedian Tim Young having a gun pointed at him on the streets of Washington, DC as he walked to a coffee shop. Bystanders did nothing but watch as he was "tossed around" and mugged. It made him feel defenseless and he consequently decided to pursue a concealed carry permit. He reported that he had, for years, been visiting locations which others regarded as 'bad places' and began to assume that nothing would ever happen. But then it did.

The left uses psychological politics to discourage you from keeping and bearing arms. Psychological politics is the act of attacking the political opposition as having pathetic psychological problems. The left characterizes carrying a gun, or even just owning a gun, as a symptom of maladjustment, of paranoia, as if there are no criminals, no threats anywhere.

And so we ask, who has the psychological problem? Who is paranoid and living in an imaginary world? Who has a responsible, adult account of reality? Who is inordinately paranoid about lawful gun ownership despite evidence of a net positive effect?

The modern media is in the business of telling us what our experience 'really means.' But there is nothing psychologically healthy about letting someone else tell you what our collective, and your individual experience, really means. Some of us see that we are a fragile form of life in need of defending itself. The left finds this conclusion so uncomfortable that it must suppress it not only in its own membership but in the whole political and social environment. Facing the dangerous nature of the world as it really is, requires a responsible, adult response. It forces us to wrestle with the threat and this takes courage. It is easier to just deny that the threat exists.

"The outcome of facing reality is confidence and life-affirming success."

What is implied by the adult response to reality, to our perfectly rational conclusion that the meaning of our experience is that we live in a dangerous world? The rational response is discipline, training, and planning. Deniers, people who choose to ignore the possibility of being threatened, are avoiding emotional discomfort and work. They do not understand that the outcome of facing reality is confidence and life-affirming success. Yes, we are happier when we are prepared for the real world. Maybe denial is just the foremost expression of laziness and the incapacity to deal with even small quantities of stress. After rejecting denial, the next step is accept the implications of this. We need to get prepared.

Most of us would agree with the military experts that it is irresponsible to let troops face combat without training. But why? Part of the answer that common sense supplies is "They won't know what to do." The other half of the answer, supplied by common sense as well as the experts, is "If they aren't trained, they will freeze under pressure. When the threat is intense, all most of us can remember and do and is what we were trained to do."

"If you are going to defend yourself, why not do it as effectively as possible?"

We are not comparing self-defense by a private citizen to aggressive combat by military personnel on search and destroy missions. It is your right, not a privilege to keep and bear arms and defend yourself, trained or untrained. Our point is simple and limited. If you are going to defend yourself, why not do it as effectively as possible? Why not reduce the odds of making disastrous mistakes which will turn you into the criminal?

The challenge of high stress situations is that they lock up our higher intellectual functions, our ability to analyze a situation, to reason our way through it, and come up with a solution to it. High threat situations cause us to forget what we only know in an intellectual sense, as opposed to being a part of our muscle memory – the kinds of memory that do not require us to *consciously* retrieve what we need to understand and operate on.

It is pretty obvious that the theory behind training for high stress situations, and combat situations in particular, is that we must reason our way through them ahead of time, decide how to handle them ahead of time (what the relevant tactics are), and then train those decisions into our memory to the point where it is all easily retrieved even when our memory wants to lock up on us.

Of course the disadvantage of memorizing responses, decisions we have already made with a trainer, about how to handle a class of situations, is that every situation is unique. We wonder if our training might lead us astray one day because it has classified situations and provided rules, operations, for dealing with those classes as such. No one has the time or resources to train for every contingently possible and unique threat situation.

We can decide to forgo training on the grounds that our experience will always be unique. But this would be irrational. Our experience as a whole, meaning the experience of trainers, military personnel, and other seasoned civilians, tells us that we are going to adapt to the uniqueness of a situation more quickly and more effectively by approaching it as a class of situation we have been trained for. A lot, if not all of our training will apply, even though the situation is unique.

Take, for example, home invasion. There are only so many contingently possible situations, and yet each one will still be unique. Apart from the details which make the situation unique (e.g. where the lamp could get in the way, whether the defender is night vision capable), the family is either upstairs, or both upstairs and downstairs. The intruders are either coming in one way or another, through one part of the house or another. We can classify and train for many different home invasion situations. The probability of one of them applying to your situation is high. Of course, the most efficient training is training for the situations that you, given your life style, are most likely to experience.

Above all else, training – having decided ahead of time what you are willing to do and what you will do – gives you a fighting chance. Your odds of surviving if not coming out on top of a serious threat, most people would agree, is dramatically increased by training.

"There is no point in carrying a weapon if one is unwilling to use it."

When someone joins the military, and specifically a combat unit, one has, in all probability, already decided what one is willing to do given a threat. One has already decided that one is in the business of eliminating threats using deadly force. This may involve killing people. There is no point in carrying a weapon, and being trained, sometimes at substantial expense, in how to use it, if one is unwilling to use it. There is no time to decide when the threat is full blown, whether or not you are really willing to use your weapon. This decision, along with many others, has to be made ahead of time. Are you willing to use your weapon to eliminate a threat to *you*? Are you willing to use your weapon to eliminate a threat to *another*? If you are not decisive ahead of time, especially about this question of whether you are willing to use your weapon in defense of another, you might be better off knowing ahead of time that you are *not* going to get personally involved. Remember, you do not have a duty to protect the other. It is grace. You have a duty to make sure the other can protect himself, if he so chooses. You might have a rule you live by like "I will defend myself and my family, but not a stranger. I will call the police, but I will not get involved personally." This rule might keep you from making some very profound mistakes that could lead to disaster for you personally, and maybe even for the person you would have otherwise defended. If you have not clearly decided, ahead of time, what you are willing, and then *able* to do, you have created a higher risk situation for yourself. And the situation is already inherently high risk. If you are not *able* to defend someone else effectively, insuring your own legal security, then you should not be willing.

During the Vietnam war, according to some reports, the American draftees had to be strongly encouraged to actually shoot to kill. As draftees, they were in theatre involuntarily. It was not a personal decision on their part to go to war, to eliminate the threat, to kill anyone. Of course, it was different whenever the threat became more personal, closer, more real. When our armed forces became professional, when our soldiers became volunteers like the marines in Iraq and Afghanistan, apparently things were different. Our officers in the field did not have order our troops to shoot to kill. This decision to eliminate the threat with deadly force had been made voluntarily which is to say, it was really a *decision*. It was made ahead of time. It is not a decision to kill people. It is a decision to eliminate the threat using force. Without that decision, already made, combat troops cannot be effective.

Part of training is to be confronted by decisions which you must make ahead of time. If you are going to engage in self-defense of any kind, let alone use deadly force to do it, you must be willing, and then able. Training is not just about being able. Being able is useless if you are not willing. You must decide what you are willing to do.

We talked to a police officer many years ago, who felt that carry laws are a joke. He took the position that people who choose to carry guns are unwilling to use them. This is the kind of ignorance that other police officers regret in a few of their brethren. It has been demonstrated historically, over and over again, that average Americans are in fact willing to use their gun to eliminate a threat. Even if this was true in only the most dramatic situations where, say, children are threatened and a parent instinctively and aggressively eliminates the threat, it would make the enabling of self-defense well worth it. This expert notion that non-experts are unwilling, that carry laws are making average people able, but not willing, is not true. As John Lott and other researchers have said and written many times in the last couple of decades, guns are used countless times each year in America to defend life and limb. Many times the trigger had to be pulled and was pulled.

What we fear as trainers, is not that people are unwilling in the end to pull the trigger, but that their decision about what they are willing to do, what they will do, given a threat, is not clear and specific enough.

This is where experts can help – even to the extent of helping you understand exactly *what* you must decide, which decisions must be made, yea or nay. For clearly, the decision that you must make as you choose to carry a gun and become able to use it effectively, safely, is not to kill people, but *eliminate threats.* The carry license is not a license to assassinate. Assassination may be a military mission. It is not a civilian mission. Once the threat is

> ***"In order to eliminate the threat you will have to shoot and shoot to kill. This does not mean that you have to insist on killing."***

eliminated, you must stop. This decision is the practical implementation of a moral doctrine, a legal doctrine, and a training, or effectiveness doctrine.

It is effective and to the point to eliminate the threat and then stop. The trainers will teach you what it means to eliminate the threat and then stop. It is not going to be a matter of shooting to wound rather than kill. That is not the point. Most trainers will insist that the worst thing you can do, under pressure, is imagine ahead of time, or at the time, that you are going to eliminate the threat with fancy shooting which only wounds. When you pull your gun, or at least the trigger, it must because deadly force is already justified legally and morally, *and is clearly required tactically*. You then proceed to use the deadly force. But the point is not to make sure the assailant is dead, but that the threat is eliminated. In order to eliminate the threat you will have to shoot and shoot to kill. This does not mean that you have to insist on killing. The law says, that once the threat is eliminated, you must stop. We make our pre-situational decisions in a legal context. This is where protecting ourselves legally begins. We have already decided, beforehand, that we will pull the trigger when deadly force is already justified, and we will stop as soon as the threat is eliminated.

No one is denying that whether or not the threat has been eliminated is a judgment call. But then, even here, training in the symptoms of a neutralized threat become extremely important. There is work to do – psychological work in establishing a willingness to do what you have the right to do and no more, and biomechanical work which enables you to do it.

CHAPTER 2

DURING THE THREAT

Obviously one could write volumes about the psychology of a fight or flight situation, and the ultimate decision to fight. The causes and management of fear are complicated. But one thing we know for sure, based on experience which goes back thousands of years: training is the major factor in managing the stress, including the fear, of the threat situation. Training induces an attitude of success, of confidence that the situation can be dealt with effectively. It increases morale during stress to the point where it is peaceful just to know that you have a fighting chance.

This book is not a substitute for that hands on training. It is an argument leading to the conclusion that you should get that training – training which deals in time and space with both what you are both *willing* and *able* to do, where these two factors, willingness and ability, cannot be separated logically, psychologically, or physically.

"Training is the major factor in managing the stress, including the fear, of the threat situation."

During the threat, as a high stress situation in which you could die or experience significant physical harm, your higher intellectual functions will not have the time, or be supplied the energy by your body, to solution the situation strategically (with a set of rules). The situation is happening. This is no time to start analyzing why it happened, whether or not it had to happen, how it could be reversed, how it could have been avoided in the first place. It may be that mistakes have already been made. Perhaps you never should have gone to the shopping mall in the first place. It's too late. All there is time for now, is tactics, not strategy.

It is not that your trainers will have nothing to say about strategy. They will have plenty to say about it. They will tell you how to avoid the tactical situation in the first place. They may help you secure your home in a fashion which is so discouraging to criminals that they will always pass you by. Experts will train you to withdraw when you can do so safely, when this does not require you to leave others unprotected in case you feel responsible for their safety. There is plenty of self-defense strategy to hash over – the kind of training, willingness, and capacity which prevents threat situations or guarantees a lot more control over them than you would otherwise have.

But it is the psychology of the *tactical* situation which is so very important as you carry a gun on a regular basis in public.

To begin with, we might suppose that, psychologically, even under stress, people can remember and apply a really fundamental classification of threat classes and levels with rules for responding appropriately. Perhaps this can be done reflexively. The simpler this matrix of threat classifications, levels, and responses is, the more useful it becomes. We have to keep things as simple as possible to start with to function under stress.

A Basic Threat Matrix

	Sample Events	Response
Nascent *Yellow*	Suspicious behavior *or* Aggressive behavior *or* Verbal threats *with* Clear disparate force[1]	Observe carefully **Get into position** **Warn others** Call the police if possible
Developing *Orange*	A weapon is unconcealed *or* the perp's body is readied for violence *or* The perp is approaching *or* The perp is declaring intent	**Draw your gun and grip it properly** Warn the threat **Be aware of the background** **Try to withdraw if possible**
Mature *Red*	A weapon is being aimed at a potential victim (you or another) *or* The perp is within close proximity	Aim the gun Assess the background Warn if there is time If the warning is ignored, shoot

1. 'Disparity of force' refers to a situation in which an aggressor possesses a distinct advantage, whether in terms of physical ability or other variables, and one would be unlikely to be able to resolve threats posed by him without recourse to deadly force.

The obvious problem with simple devices like a basic threat matrix is that it cannot capture the all-important detail inherent in your unique situation. It simply tries to convey three threat level thresholds which a developing and very dangerous situation inevitably crosses.

There is not much difference between the direct threat and the 'sheep dog' threat where you have decided to aid another. In deciding to protect someone else, you have decided to identify with him or her, and now you are putting yourself in their place and performing as if they were performing for themselves. One difference is that it might be tactically effective not to show your gun until the last moment. Otherwise giving the perpetrator a warning and an opportunity to withdraw is ideal.

Now imagine how complicated our matrix could become if we started to add detail relative to a given environment. We would edit the events and responses for the home environment, the office environment, the street or outdoor environment, the public indoor environment, and so on. This thought experiment – the construction of detailed threat matrix – is useful only because it demonstrates that such a device could never be consciously applied during a high stress situation in a unique, relative environment. To put it another way, consciously applying a complex rule set to a situation is a higher intellectual function. Our response in a fight which may materialize almost instantly must be relevant, effective, and reflexive. In other words, the response has to be instinctive, subconscious.

If this is our psychological premise then we need to distinguish between a higher intellectual function like applying complex rules to complex situations and the subconscious application of *technique* to a broad range of situations. Applying rules, and applying technique, are two different things.

In effect, in this chapter, we have asked ourselves the following question: Can we *program* ourselves to follow a complex set of rules for dealing with a large set of possible situations so our application of them is analogous to how a computer instantly applies complex business rule sets to a very large array of business events?

We think the answer to this question is "No." The reason why we invented computer technology is precisely because it is not possible for human beings to apply complex rules sets to complex events *instantaneously*. This is a fantasy.

The relevance of rules as such is relative to a situation. Absolute rules will often be rendered inapplicable or even dangerous by the situation in which we find ourselves. For example, it cannot be a hard and fast rule that you always show your gun or even warn a perp before you use it. There may not be time. It might be bad tactics, subjecting you or someone you are defending to more risk.

None of your trainers can or should be constructing a complex set of rules for

> ***"Self-defense, practically speaking, is the reflexive, subconscious application of broad principles and proven technique."***

alternative situations and asking you to memorize them and apply them rigorously in a high stress situation. Instead, what you can apply are principles and technique. We do not believe it is appropriate to think of self-defense training as being anchored in rule sets which we must train the brain to apply instantly. The correct premise is that self-defense, practically speaking, is the reflexive, subconscious application of broad principles and proven technique.

Although you cannot, on average, in a high stress situation, consciously apply a complicated set of rules to an event which you must first analyze in order to decide which rules are relevant, you can be taught to consistently hold and even aim a gun properly *and subconsciously*, under pressure. And if this is true, then even the most basic training in using a gun to defend yourself, is pure gold. The right training focuses on universal principles (not specific rule sets for specific events) and technique. *What this means to you is that the essential training, the relevant training, will not, cannot, cost you more time and money than you can afford.*

When we analyze the psychology of self-defense, we arrive at the conclusion that we must focus on *principles* of response and on technique. This focus is precisely what makes your training manageable as well as essential. In other words, basic training has tremendous value – the bulk of the value you can realize from training. Everyone can afford and access that much training. More training will add value but the returns, compared to the basic training, probably diminish. If the price of your *basic* gun training was actually value-based, it would cost an arm and a leg. All subsequent training would become, relatively speaking, of less and less value and therefore cheaper and cheaper. But this is not the way the gun training industry works and you should take full advantage of this. The basic gun training you can get today, focusing on principles for responding, and technique, is an incredible buy.

During the threat, panic is avoided by training you can actually apply, reflexively, subconsciously. This is training which is focused on both *principles* and *techniques* which are universally relevant. We will start your training in these principles and techniques in Part Three.

CHAPTER 3

AFTER THE THREAT

After your training has helped you eliminate a threat, you still have to keep your head screwed on good and tight. This is because the immediate aftermath of a shooting incident will have a great deal to do with the legal landscape. You need to do the landscaping. You have to be in calculated control of how you shape the situation, after you have gotten past your fear of being injured or killed. Now you have to deal intelligently with the fear of being prosecuted – in effect, of being *misunderstood* or understood and exploited anyway by an officer looking for a good collar. Do not assume the police are on your side. This is a big mistake. There are former police officers and prosecutors who will tell you not to say anything, ever, to the police (at least absent a lawyer) because they have ways of using almost anything you say to pursue a line of reasoning leading to an arrest and indictment. You could be talking about the weather and some detective, who gets paid for being suspicious, will find something suspect to pursue. This is no time for a casual conversation.

"You have to be in calculated control of how you shape the situation, after you have gotten past your fear of being injured or killed."

Assuming you have defended yourself legally, you must make sure that what has happened is not misunderstood either by the police or the bystanders they will interview. You started your defense when you warned the assailant not to hurt either you or the other and then stopped shooting when the threat was eliminated. It was clear that you were not the aggressor, but the potential victim. Now, the aftermath, might be a more stressful situation than the gunfight. We will cover the legal process of defending yourself in more detail in Part 4 of this book.

"You will remain calm because your training has already taught you that you need not do a lot of talking. The less the better."

Under stress, you can screw up your responses to the police without training. Here again, you need training, and you need to follow it instinctively after you have defended yourself with a gun.

Your gun is back in its holster (don't put it somewhere else) and your hands are in the air when the cops get there. In the meantime you remain calm. You have to. You will remain calm because of your training. Above all else, you will remain calm because your training has already taught you that you need not do a lot of talking. The less the better.

This is not the time to lay out the whole story. You and your lawyer can do that later. You do not start spewing out a long-winded narrative under stress.

After you have eliminated the threat you have not acted crazy and you have not said anything about the threat. You have not kicked him, or sworn at him, or suggested in any way that the violence became personal or that you are aggressive. It is the other guy who was aggressive. Your behavior is responsible.

The calm you need after the threat has been eliminated, the psychology of it, comes from the knowledge that you need not and should not be putting any pressure on yourself to tell your story, your narrative, under stress. The only thing you need to do is make it clear that you were attacked. Then you wait for your lawyer.

Oh. You haven't planned ahead for legal support? Now that will stress you out. After you have defended yourself with a gun, your calm, minimalist response to the police will rely on whether or not you have the card in your billfold with the phone number of the concealed carry insurance company you have wisely contracted with. This is the card with the phone number which you can call to have a lawyer at your disposal, twenty-four hours a day, who knows the laws under which you will be reviewed, and knows exactly how to defend you.

After the threat is gone, a new threat arises instantly – the threat of prosecution and a civil law suit. You have to train and prepare for the aftermath just as you train and prepare for the event proper. The aftermath is potentially more difficult and challenging than the self-defense event. If you are prepared, it will be much less stressful and much more positive in its outcome.

The preparation for the aftermath, which keeps you calm and effective in your own defense, is very likely to make you more effective *during* the fight. Knowing that you are prepared for the aftermath will make you more likely to go ahead and defend yourself or another legally. As you assess the situation, knowing that you are prepared for the consequences of

> ***"Ability, willingness, principles, technique, legal preparation. These are attributes of a citizen who cannot be victimized."***

protecting yourself will go a long way in refusing to become a victim. After all, what this is all about is refusing to become a helpless victim. If this is not about encouraging you to go ahead and defend yourself legally, then what is it about?

Knowing that you are not only prepared for the fight in front of you, but also for the fight which follows it, will help you stay calm: before, during, and after the application of deadly force. Ability, willingness, principles, technique, legal preparation. These are attributes of a citizen who cannot be victimized.

In summary, your decision to defend yourself, which is your God-given right, and to train and prepare, induces *confidence.* And when both the bystanders and the police see confidence, instead of doubt and fear, you have already made the most important statement you can possibly make to both the witnesses and the police. The guilty are nervous and distraught. The innocent are confident.

CHAPTER 4

SUMMARY

CONFIDENCE: THE PRODUCT OF TRAINING AND PREPARATION

We can summarize our view of the psychology of self-defense with a formula:

Willingness + ability + capacity (your weapon)
+ training + preparation
= readiness
= confidence and responsibility.

Confidence and responsibility go hand in hand.

We dream of an America in which tens of millions of citizens, not subjects, are confidently armed and ready at all times. This has clear implications for the psychology of criminals, including terrorists. It is very, very inhibiting. Not to be sexist, but in particular we envision a country full of women who are treated in a consistently civilized and polite fashion by everyone because of their confidence, *because they are ready.* They have become responsible for their own defense. They have become strong.

"Confidence and responsibility go hand in hand."

Learning to defend yourself, being ready, induces a level of confidence which will benefit you in every department of your life, including work. Carrying a gun is part of a whole lifestyle which is marked with confidence *and responsibility.* You cannot take care of other people, until you are confidently taking care of yourself. We all have to decide if we are going to be the strong one, or the weak one who has to be defended by others. Life is much more interesting and satisfying when we decide to be strong and confident. This will cost you. You will have to take care of others, hopefully without enabling them to be dependent without a good excuse. We should not long to be the one who has to be defended. We should become the one who provides the defense. If you cannot defend yourself, first and foremost, you cannot defend anyone else.

The training, once again, is an incredible buy. The return on investment is huge. If it does not save your life, or that of another, it may give you the confidence which prevents even modest forms of aggression from interrupting your life. Years of bear hunting has convinced us that bears can smell the confidence of someone carrying a gun. It is an instinct. Predatory animals are triggered by fear. We would not be surprised if human predators are inhibited by the same subconscious perception of confidence in someone who is simply ready, even when this readiness is concealed. Criminals, paradoxically, are not usually looking for trouble. They are looking for victims who make it easy. They wait until they smell a lack of confidence. Crime feeds on the absence of confidence. It is functional. The less confident you are, the more confident the criminal becomes.

Confidence is the summarizing psychological concept. All of your training and preparation is leading to confidence, before, during, and after the presentation of a serious threat. As we move forward we will address the details of the elements of confidence. For example, part of the formula noticed above is capacity. Capacity is your weapon and your ammunition. Knowing yourself, the constraints and opportunities in your life-style with respect to consistently carrying a gun, is a prime example of how you realize the formula, how you tweak it to maximize your readiness and your confidence. There is such a thing as the right gun, or at least the right class of firearm, for your ability level, your training level, your lifestyle, your willingness to use it. An unwieldy gun, and an unwieldy way of carrying it, can be very damaging to your readiness and your confidence. Sweating a little detail up front pays huge dividends for the rest of your life. The whole formula has to be realized, not a just a part of it.

"Hopefully you will never have to draw your gun. The odds of having to do so go down as your confidence goes up."

As we move forward we are not leaving the psychology of self-defense behind. We are not done with the formula. It is time to customize the formula for you. Only you can do this. But you need the information we will give you here and good hands on training, to realize the formula in your life, which you have already decided is worth defending. You can defend your whole life, its whole impact on you and others, by simply being confident. Hopefully you will never have to draw your gun. The odds of having to do so go down as your confidence goes up. As your confidence grows, your whole life gets better.

> ***"Bullies do not have confidence. They live in fear and insecurity."***

Do not be a victim. If you refuse to be a victim bodily, in this concrete corporeal sense, you will probably start refusing to be a victim in any sense. In the meantime, the confidence will also make you gracious. Bullies do not have confidence. They live in fear and insecurity. We do not want you to live in fear and insecurity. Fear destroys grace. Your confidence, based on your readiness, is the foundation of your grace under fire – both literally and figuratively.

PART 3

INTRODUCTION TO THE PRINCIPLES AND TECHNIQUES OF SELF-DEFENSE WITH A HANDGUN

CHAPTER 1

WHICH GUN? WHICH GEAR?

In this section, our discussion of technique will help you understand how the confidence formula has to be customized for you. Your choice of technology and the biomechanics of using it (e.g. drawing it and aiming it) are inextricable.

If your equipment does not fit your lifestyle and biomechanics, it will become an uncomfortable burden to use it, to go into the world equipped and ready. If you are not comfortable with your gun, and the way you carry it, your confidence level will deteriorate. You will be more successful in integrating concealed carry into your life, making it a consistent practice that ensures capacity when the time comes, if you reconcile your gear to your lifestyle instead of changing your lifestyle for your gear.

We are not saying that self-defense is not a change, an evolution, in your way of life, benefiting both you and your neighbors. We are saying that the more you can alter your gear, rather than your habitual way of living, the more likely you are to have the capacity – the great equalizer – on your person, when the event you may not be expecting forces itself on you.

"Reconcile your gear to your lifestyle instead of changing your lifestyle for your gear."

For example, a runner, who spends a large portion of his life in running shorts and a t-shirt, will need to adjust his carry equipment to that way of life. There are fanny pack holsters and very light weight guns and gun holders (so small that "holster" is not the right word) to accommodate athletic clothing. A woman who wears skirts more often than pants will have to consider the best way to conceal a weapon given her wardrobe. A man who wears suit coats or jackets consistently may be able to conceal a larger frame handgun which actually fits his hand.

Obviously there are even more fundamental conditions which must be fed into your decisions about gear. Body size and/or strength will affect your ability to manage recoil. Drawing a small gun out of an inside the belt holster takes a bit more dexterity than drawing a larger frame pistol from a holster at your side.

It becomes clear, very quickly, that you need some place where you can experience the options. Fortunately, the variety of guns and other equipment that you can choose from is wider than ever.

Here are some variables which should be considered as you choose your gun and its caliber.

- Hand size and dexterity
- Wrist and arm strength
- Overall weight/body size (recoil management)
- Body shape
- Eye conditions like presbyopia or near-sightedness
- Wardrobe (as determined by lifestyle)

If your belly hangs over your belt, your best holster option is not inside the belt, next to your belly button. It might be a shoulder holster right under your armpit. But many experts will tell you this will slow down your draw compared to a holster worn on the side.

There are plenty of choices which you will have to make. One of them is to have enough alternative equipment to deal with different kinds of public appearances. It can get expensive to gear up for all of the kinds of clothes and situations which you find yourself in. So the most fundamental decision is how many carry guns you want to own. One gun means that your wardrobe options are limited. Several guns allow you to wear whatever you wish.

Many people can only afford one gun, and one holster. If so, that gun will have to work summer and winter, with more or less clothing. Many experienced permit holders will tell you that the gun they consistently carry, because of its convenience, is a very small frame .380 caliber pistol. A good example of this is the Smith and Wesson 'Bodyguard.' Some experts will condemn carrying a gun in your pocket, but there is simply no question that a gun you can slip into your pocket will be carried much more consistently than a larger gun which has to be holstered. The substantial disadvantage of a small gun is its small magazine. The typical .380 caliber handgun uses magazines that are limited to six rounds.

We are at the point where we can describe a kind of natural law associated with concealed carry. The law is that the more determined you are to carry consistently, the more likely you will gravitate to a small frame gun as your most utilized option. This is in turn raises the most important question about habitual concealed carry: Are you going to develop the habit of using a holster or not?

The Smith & Wesson Bodyguard 380: a small-frame, lightweight, easily-concealed pistol.

Carrying a small-frame gun in your pocket or purse is very convenient, but is it tactically effective? It is certainly better than nothing, but any mode of carry other than a real holster can catch on your small gun, or settle it into an adverse position. The slide on the top of your gun is the heaviest part of the gun and will turn it upside down in your pocket or purse as you move. This makes it difficult to draw your gun quickly, position it in front of your eyes, and acquire your target. We would rather draw against a perpetrator dragging a gun out of his pocket than one drawing from a waist holster.

And so the natural law we have already mentioned is joined by a functional reality. The consistency with which you carry a small-frame gun may result in suboptimizing the *way* you carry it. We recommend one small discipline, one stern rule to apply to your consistent carry of a small frame handgun: Carry it in some kind of holster on your body if at all possible. There are many options for men and women wearing pants, less for women wearing dresses. It is easy to go inside the belt with a small-frame gun. It is obviously even easier to conceal a holstered small-frame handgun beneath a coat than a holstered large-frame gun, and it is more comfortable by weight and dimensions.

There are purses designed to carry a gun in the proper position for a faster draw. There are fanny packs which do the same. If you google 'concealed carry clothing' and 'concealed carry holsters' you will find plenty of information we do not need to catalog here.

Assuming that you get squared away with respect to both how often you carry (consistently) and how you carry (in a holster) the small frame handgun confronts you with one more very important choice. Small-frame guns like the .380 caliber have very small magazines. Most will only hold six rounds. So, if at all possible, you should carry a backup magazine when you carry a small-frame gun. Fortunately, the magazines are so small, it is easy to carry one or more of them. Again, these magazines should be carried in a fashion which makes it easy to find them and quickly position them for insertion into the handle of your pistol. There are holsters for extra magazines and you should use them if you are wearing a belt or a waist band. Many purses designed for carry, and fanny packs, have a place to keep extra magazines where they can be easily retrieved. But to begin with you should maximize the number of rounds in your pistol by loading one into the chamber with a full magazine in the handle of the gun. This means, for example, that a .380 caliber which typically holds six rounds in its magazine, plus one in the chamber, gives you seven shots. The seventh could save your life.

Carrying one or more spare magazines, and drilling in rapidly and safely changing them under stress, doubles or triples your available firepower.

In summary, there are a few laws or principles you will find operating inside of your concealed carry habits.

1. As the size and weight of your carry gun goes down, the consistency with which you carry it will go up. This is a central tendency, not a rule: many licensees have, through long practice, become very proficient at carrying a medium- or large-frame gun, and do so consistently.
2. As the size and weight of your gun goes down, the more likely it becomes that you will carry it unholstered. This central tendency is to be resisted.
3. As the size and weight of your gun goes down, you will be more likely to use a holster, instead of your pocket or purse,

if you have one or more which easily slips on and off of your belt, or is otherwise very easy to attach and detach. This principle is particularly relevant to a male wardrobe.

4. As the size and weight of your gun goes down, the more backup magazines you should be carrying.

> **"A lot of gun ranges have very helpful people who will direct you to the right rental guns to compare."**

Keep in mind that there may be a price to pay in recoil for this natural tendency to small-frame pistols for carry. Large-frame guns do not kick as much when shooting the same calibers, for example 9mm and .380. Recoil is based on weight to caliber (including the powder charge, light or hot). You should practice with the gun you carry, so this is an important consideration. You may have to deal with a marginally larger amount of recoil with a small-frame gun shooting a smaller caliber bullet. A small-frame .380 may jump more in your hand than a .45 1911 handgun. You will have to rent a few guns at the local range and see how they compare. In fact, this is an essential part of the process as you head toward carrying a handgun on a consistent basis. A large-frame 9mm may not put as much stress on your wrist as a 9mm small-frame pistol. And getting back on target will be faster, with less recoil. There is no strictly linear reduction in recoil as you move to small cartridges in small guns. There are no clear, published functions that we know of which tell us that *felt* recoil, as you reduce both the caliber of the bullet and the frame size of the gun, are perfectly offsetting. You may experience a marginal increase in felt recoil as you move from a medium frame 9mm to a small frame .380. It does not take that much time to find out. A lot of gun ranges have very helpful people who will direct you to the right rental guns to compare.

You can avoid a lot of buyer's remorse by taking just one afternoon to try out half a dozen rental handguns. You are unique. Avoid the dogmatists on this question of which gun will work for you as a tool you will consistently carry.

Choose a pistol whose slide you can comfortably rack, both when routinely charging the firearm and when clearing stoppages.

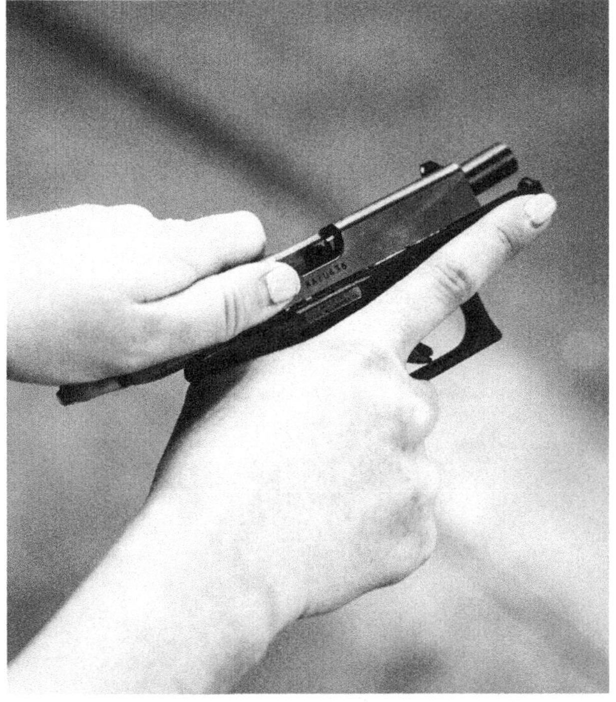

CHAPTER 2

UNUSUAL METHODS OF CARRY

We categorize carry in a holster at the waist, on or near the belly, or under the arm, in a purse, or in fanny pack, as 'standard'. Other types of carry are non-standard for the purposes of this book.

Why would you need a non-standard form of carry such as inside the thigh, in the small of your back, or on your ankle? Because your job, recreation, or wardrobe demand it. It really comes down to what you wear as a consequence of what you have to do or choose to do. And this is ironic because your wardrobe is not, in our opinion, and even in a lady's case, a good justification for wearing your gun where it will be very difficult to draw. This difficulty will also suppress your commitment to practicing your draw from non-standard carry positions. Many ranges, even outside ranges, will not allow you to draw from these non-standard holster locations. *They may not allow you to practice your draw at all.*

"It really comes down to what you wear as a consequence of what you have to do or choose to do."

Some ranges will qualify you for draw practice, but it is unlikely that they will ever allow you to practice a non-standard draw. You are going to have to do that in the woods or at a gravel pit. And someone should always be with you, because you are much more likely to pass the muzzle of the gun over parts of your own body.

School teachers who are allowed to carry their guns, concealed, at school, to protect their students, are the best example we can think of where we may be forced to compromise some draw efficiency to accommodate the wardrobe. In schools, the authorities want the guns well-concealed, and they want their teachers

"it is essential that teachers keep their weapons a very secure secret, even while they are wearing them."

wearing mainstream clothes. This supports a policy of the students never knowing who is carrying so potential attackers cannot target them. The whole program is a brilliant way to keep a kid who is sick enough to plan mayhem off balance. There is no point in attempting to commit this kind of crime if there is a very good chance of failing. Failure in this arena does not lead so much to infamy as it does to ridicule.

In a school where the teachers are carrying, and no one really knows who or how many, the objective of any school shooter becomes much more difficult to achieve. The whole point is to realize carnage. In order to be much more sure of achieving his goal the terrorist will be very likely to move on to another target. As soon as teachers are carrying their guns, every day at school, from coast to coast, we will see a dramatic reduction in school shootings and, perhaps, a dramatic and reciprocal increase in mall and theatre shootings. It is absolutely clear that school shooters are not just irritated at their schools, but are operating on a soft target. It's both.

If our budding terrorist knows which teachers are armed and which are not, perhaps because nearly everyone knows, he may be tempted to work around this hazard. So it is essential that teachers keep their weapons a very secure secret, even while they are wearing them, and this may require holster locations which are difficult to draw from. If the teachers start wearing some kind of uniform (the students see a trend toward loose or bulky clothes among a subset of teachers), kids will be smart enough to figure out who has the guns.

It is important to figure this all out, because we want trained, law-abiding teachers to carry their pistols at school and shoot down, with prejudice, anyone who arrives at their school to kill their kids. We have to make it work.

David Brooks of the NY Times (among others and as the representative for all others of this ilk) has asserted that letting teachers carry concealed firearms at school is 'demented'. Either Mr. Brooks' assertion is a completely subjective and relative judgment which, as such, is not worth sustained attention, or he has an *argument* in mind, where an argument is always an attempt to universalize one's conclusions by use of implicating premises which are sound and widely shared. Mr. Brooks owes us a clear, logically valid syllogism. We do not expect him to be an analytic philosopher. But, given his vocation, we do expect him to perform at a somewhat more sophisticated level than he has sunk to in imputing dementia to so many willing teachers.

What could the implicit syllogism be? Major Premise: It is madness when teachers offer more than conventional instruction in the classroom. Minor Premise: Protecting kids with a gun is something more than offering conventional instruction in the classroom. Therefore: It is demented to let teachers protect kids with a gun.

Now obviously, the major premise is just stupid – a judgment we believe is more universal than those of Mr. Brooks'. The value added by teachers almost always exceeds their instruction in the classroom (they are coaches and mentors, friends and extant protectors in many regards) and we have rarely if ever considered this intrinsically mad. Most of us do not think it was 'demented' for those teachers who have sacrificed themselves in past shootings to do so. Mr. Brooks apparently believes that these heroes *were* demented even though they were obviously effective.

David Brooks cannot successfully position his radically relative judgments as if they are themselves sound, intuitive, and popular starting points. His ilk is getting nowhere questioning the judgments of millions of Americans which do not align with his own. Otherwise intelligent people become all too puerile as soon as they see a bulge under the clothing of a law-abiding citizen.

We take it Mr. Brooks, as our representative plaintiff, thinks it is demented for concealed carry permit holders to protect themselves and other people *outside* of the educational arena. If not, what is the difference? Permit holders should shoot down terrorists, teenagers nonetheless, in places of business as well as schools, as the truly demented try to murder the flower, or the fruit, of the nation. Is this response insane or is the insanity in Mr. Brooks' theatrical judgments? For a commentator who works so hard at sustaining a moderate image, his immoderate drama-mongering would be surprising if it were not such a familiar habit of those who have turned the gun into a fetish which is possessed by an evil spirit, determines evil action unilaterally, and requires religious, if not hysterical exorcism. Brooks has always hungered for the respect and affection of the media elites. His identification with the most mediocre souls on earth is, apparently, earned.

All by way of defending the common sense of the many teachers who own guns and encouraging them to proceed with a brave and selfless program of protecting the students they love with a gun they know how to conceal and wield.

There are several types of 'unusual carry/non-carry' to discuss:

a. In the Boot or on the Ankle
b. Shoulder Holster
c. The Small of the Back
d. Inside the Thigh
e. In a Secure Drawer or Container
f. In a Purse or Pack

We would classify carry inside the belt and right under the belly button as a standard way of carrying. There are many good holsters designed for this. There are a plethora of holsters designed for carry at the side of the waist. Your options for 'unusual' carry are more limited.

(A) IN THE BOOT OR ON THE ANKLE

'In the boot' means in some kind of holster that fits into the boot or in an ankle holster covered by a boot. This is a great place to conceal even a larger frame pistol, but has two major drawbacks. First, it requires you to wear big boots. Second, raising the pant leg and then reaching into the boot for the weapon takes time and may lead to the gun being hung up on the boot or your pants.

We do not understand why anyone would add the complexity, the inhibition of the boot, to a standard ankle holster. Covering an ankle holster with something other than skinny jeans (the pants leg should be as loose as possible) is better than covering it with a boot. Just lift the pants leg and draw the weapon.

"Not being able to find or wield anything important, under pressure, can stress us out very quickly."

Carrying a gun in a boot without a holster is a last resort. It's perfectly obvious that the gun will sink as far into the boot as it can, and getting it out under pressure could become too time-consuming and increase your stress. And this is a very important point. In an emergency, if it suddenly becomes difficult to find and draw your gun, the stress will go exponential. We all know this from analogous experiences. Not being able to find or wield anything important, under pressure, can stress us out very quickly. On the other hand, being able to instantly acquire your gun, and grip it properly will also instantly suggest to your medulla oblongata that you have some control. This is calming. It seems like a very small thing but, psychologically, being in control of your weapon may be equivalent to being in control of the situation, and your subconscious will know it.

The only situation where hiding a gun in your boot even begins to make sense is when you are, for whatever strange reason, wearing such short-legged pants that they move up over your ankle holster whenever you sit down. In this case you would be using the boot to actually conceal the weapon. But this concealment problem should be solved by simply wearing longer-legged pants and monitoring the exposure of the weapon when you insist on crossing your legs. Better to adopt new sitting habits and use an ankle holster alone than use a boot without a holster, or a holster with a boot.

A lady may object that she can conceal a gun in a boot when she is wearing a dress. But in that case, concealing the weapon inside the thigh makes more sense to us than hiding it in a boot where anyone might look down into it.

(B) THE SHOULDER HOLSTER

Starting with the shoulder holster, which a female can use with a coat, it is important to consider the ease of draw. We recommend a shoulder holster which allows for pulling the pistol or revolver straight down and out where the holster retains the weapon through compression. Obviously there has to be enough compression to keep the weapon in the holster and make it hard for an attacker to withdraw. Shoulder holsters which require you to draw a gun straight out with the muzzle facing toward your body presents a greater hazard during a struggle and, in any event, the coat may get in the way of turning it around. When you pull a longer pistol down and out of a compression shoulder holster you should pull it out from under the bottom edge of the coat. This guarantees it will not get stuck in the coat. Unfortunately there is no escape from the relative inefficiency of drawing from a shoulder holster compared to drawing straight from the waist with your preferred hand. When we consider the disadvantages of a shoulder holster it suggests that you may be better off with just securing your gun in a drawer or some other authorized container if you are a teacher. The huge disadvantage of this is that you may not have the gun with you when you need it. Some schools will require that you remain in control of the weapon at all times, and this means carrying it.

(C) THE SMALL OF THE BACK

This approach to carry cannot be practically justified if a coat or shirt is still required to hide the weapon. In that case the holster may as well be moved to the hip, where most experts believe it offers the best position for drawing quickly and safely.

It is as simple as that. Carrying in the small of your back will always require concealment, just like carrying at your side, whether this means you are using a waistband or belt as a poor substitute for a real holster.

We can only think of one reason for putting the weapon in the small of your back. You might be teaching dance classes and have people's hands on your waist all day long – or something along these lines. Unless your gun is going to be detected by feel, precisely because it is on your side (which always supports the fastest and most reliable draw), keep it at your side, in a holster.

(D) INSIDE THE THIGH

There is a substantial concealment issue associated with a holster attached to the inside of the thigh for ladies. Either the dress or skirt has to be appropriately long to keep the weapon concealed, making it

> **"There are too many more practical options."**

unacceptably difficult to get to the weapon, or the risk of the weapon being detected, let alone uncomfortable while hidden under a shorter skirt, increases dramatically. Of course this difficulty may be mitigated by long skirts or dresses which open up very quickly in front of the weapon. Wearing this sort of fashion on a regular basis may be a dead giveaway. It would be better to just carry a small frame pistol in a pocket on the dress or loose fitting riding style pleated pants.

We think inside-the-thigh carry is almost out of the question. There are too many more practical options, like keeping the weapon in a purse. But if a school teacher is required to keep the weapon on her person at all times, we can imagine this option being tested. Getting separated from a purse with a gun inside of it, whether by force or forgetfulness, especially in a school, may make carrying a weapon inside of the thigh a less stressful option.

On the other hand, inside-the-thigh-carry may be very effective in convincing most people, including most students, that a female is not carrying at all. But is this such a substantial tactical advantage that it is worth the drawbacks?

Perhaps the most important drawback to consider is that inside-the-thigh is only comfortable, even possible, with a very small frame pistol with small magazines and therefore a very limited number of rounds. Whether at school, or on the street, we would recommend carrying at least twelve to fifteen rounds if at all possible. (But six or seven in a small frame .380 is better than nothing.) An inside-the-thigh holster should have a sidebar for an extra magazine. Obviously this will add weight and some additional discomfort to this option.

(E) IN A SECURE DRAWER OR CONTAINER

Whether at home or at school, a locked container is a great way to conceal and secure a gun, as long as it is easy to retrieve it. Schools may veto this option by requiring the gun to be on the person of those permitted to carry, at all times. Otherwise a small gun case which opens to a unique palm print, and can be concealed and bolted to the inside of a desk, certainly conceals the weapon and probably secures it better than when it is carried. Obviously any key for opening a gun safe should be *on* your person. If the key is locked up itself it becomes too time-consuming to get the gun safe proper open. It puts us at risk of not being able to access the gun at all. It is too easy to lose or misplace the key, or even forget its location under stress. We think the best pistol safes are the ones which will open when you use a digital sequence or a palm print. A palm print is to be preferred. It is amazing how easy it is to forget even a short series of numbers under stress. It is easy to see that the least stressful retrieval of a handgun will always be retrieving it from a holster which is right at your waist, on your body. And the advantage of this, giving you a calming sense of control, in an active shooter situation, probably outweighs every other consideration. When the situation suddenly materializes, and you instantly draw the gun from your waist holster, it tells you that you are prepared. Being prepared is a crucial source of confidence. This is a huge step forward toward eliminating the threat.

Keeping your gun in a secure container is for school, work, and home – wherever you cannot consistently carry the gun on your body, and where there are others who should not have access to the weapon. In all other environments, the gun should be on your person and ready in your waist holster.

A gym teacher will have to have a secure container, hopefully close by, for his or her gun. There is no perfect, universal tactic here for school, business, or home.

So instead, we need to think of the container option as something which should always be available in these environments, and used as the non-optimal, but necessary solution. In summary, the secure container, almost always concealed itself, is a necessary backup, and never the sufficient solution all by itself.

(F) IN THE PURSE OR PACK

The purse or pack (fanny pack et al) is, like the secure non-mobile container, an indispensable option within an overall strategy. We think of the hierarchy of solutions in the following way. First comes the holstered gun, at your waist, on your person. Second comes the weapon concealed in your purse or pack. So much the better if it is attached to your body; a gun in a purse or pack left beyond arm's reach can become as much a threat as a defense. Third comes the weapon secured in a container which it is fast and easy only for authorized personnel to open. All three options should be available at school, at the business, and even in the home.

For females, the purse or pack is preferable to any other option except the holster at the waist – the universally, gender-neutral, optimum form of carry.

CHAPTER 3

ASSESSING THE THREAT

One cable news pundit, just after the Florida school shooting in February of 2018, made the bizarre claim that a teacher's handgun would be useless against the AR-15s carried by some school shooters because the bullet of the AR-15 travels three times faster – as if the teacher should be waiting for the assailant to shoot at the exact same nanosecond when she shoots at him. One envisions our champion and the terrorist agreeing to square off for a fair duel in which she has put herself, voluntarily, at a disadvantage.

> ***"Media geniuses, as such, should not be expected to recognize what common sense reveals to the rest of us."***

Of course, one response to the pundit's silly warning is to recommend that the school defend itself with AR-15s. This would, indeed, be highly effective.

But just in case you are using a gun which uses a slower bullet, you should try to shoot first, before any terrorist even sees you. And in case he does see you and fires first, it would be best if you fired back anyway. Media geniuses, as such, should not be expected to recognize what common sense reveals to the rest of us, viz. that a slower moving bullet can still kill an assailant who is using a faster moving bullet and does so much more efficiently and reliably than weekend judo. The slower-moving bullet is not the bulk of your tactical burden. Getting into position and acting preemptively is.

One thing about a school shooting is that no one is going to doubt that the responding teacher is in fear of death or great bodily harm to her or to others. And that is the almost universal standard for assessing the threat.

But of course this is a subjective, not an objective requirement. You do not have to prove that you would have actually died, or been seriously harmed. But it may have to be clear that this would have been more likely than not. It is unlikely that law-abiding citizens are going to shoot without fearing for their lives or fearing injury, but the judge and jury are going to decide if this fear was 'reasonable'.

Two difficulties loom with this standard then, which will foreshadow our discussion in the next section of the book. There we will deal in more depth with the question of just how objective and universal a rational standard for your actions really is.

The first question about the standard is what would constitute serious injury? Just how injured do we, and the jury, have to imagine we are going to be? Does one have to be more than kicked or bruised? And if one is kicked or bruised wouldn't this reasonably induce the fear that more injury is coming? When is it reasonable to be so fearful before anything has actually happened? Since when does fear of any kind *have* to be rational? What kind of psychology is the state expecting here? And what could it mean to *prove* that I in fact had this fear of death or injury? After all, who else is in a position to deny it?

Obviously, the jury, the judge, has to see the situation as one which would normally cause justifying fear in otherwise average people. It is contingently possible that someone might authentically fear for their life when a stranger looks sideways at them, even with a smile. But here, as mere pragmatists, we know that the authorities will conclude that this is a symptom of mental illness, not the rational fear of a normal person. Most of us, during any average day, without drugs or alcohol, know how to assess a threat. When we do so, and use our guns, it better be without drugs or alcohol in our systems. We have to accept the risk of carrying only when we are sober. A rationally, soberly assessed threat is a threat which normal people would react to with fear of being killed or injured. If you know a lot of normal people, or are normal yourself, you have reliable intuitions about this standard.

> ***"If you know a lot of normal people, or are normal yourself, you have reliable intuitions."***

So to begin with, you are planning to testify honestly to the effect that you had justifying fear. Think about it. The one thing that can get someone else to doubt this, is thinking that the exact same situation would not have filled them with the same fear. Any case of self-defense, on average, will not hinge on testimony about fear alone. It must hinge on the description of the public situation – especially by other witnesses.

In that case, you must contribute to the nature of the situation while it is happening. In other words: what you do in a threatening situation is much more important than what the assailant does, both with respect to protecting yourself legally and protecting yourself and others physically.

If you have the time and opportunity you must make it clear to any bystanders, and to any cameras, that you are the victim. You must announce your fear by demanding that the assailant withdraw, by telling him not to hurt you or anyone else. You should withdraw to the extent you can (but don't turn your back on him). "Don't hurt me. Let me go. Don't hurt anyone." This sort of announcement is so natural under stress that it should not be difficult to remember to shout it out. Everyone around you will then know that you are in fact afraid and this, for them, *becomes an objective aspect of the situation they will describe as witnesses.* When asked, they will say, "Yes, the defendant was clearly afraid and said so, and asked the attacker to stop."

"Your assessment, which you are being forced to make, is that you are about to suffer death or harm if you do not act."

If you do not have the time and opportunity to make it clear that you are the victim, not the aggressor, with these verbal and behavioral signals, then it is probably because the situation is already clear by nature. In this case the assailant is so aggressive that it speaks for itself.

Otherwise, what we are suggesting here, is that you have to speak *for* the situation, because a huge part of the situation is what is going on inside of you. What is going on inside of you is going to be easy for the jury to identify with, unless you are drawing your gun on someone who is completely unarmed, of the same sex, and smaller than you.

In any event, the situation is yours to assess and you should testify to this assessment explicitly, at the time and place, if it is truly threatening. Your assessment, which you are being forced to make, is that you are about to suffer death or harm if you do not act.

When is it too late to enforce the correct perception of the situation? It is too late when the attacker is already pointing his gun, or even just unveiling it, or when he is actually approaching with the knife or club in his hand and is within seconds of arriving, or even just approaching armed only with his fists. Here, again, if he is a lot smaller than you, the judge and jury may have a problem with the non-deadly disparate force seeming to be on your side. Your best excuse for using deadly force is the adequate force of the assailant. It is adequate to cause you serious harm at a minimum.

Is it too late when the potential attacker is just issuing scary threats? No. This is when it is essential to make your fear clear. He has no right to induce this fear, to make 'terroristic threats'. He is telling you he is

"The important thing here is that his dangerous intentions, and your understanding of them as such, should also be clear to any bystander."

going to hurt you or even kill you. In that case your gun should be out and pointing at him. If he will not relent and is close enough to disarm you before you can shoot, you can try to retreat and gain some ground. After you have announced your fear and let him know that you are armed, you should not allow him to get close enough to disarm you before you can shoot. This distance will vary by your ability. The twenty-one foot rule is not an absolute. You may need more space before there is a good chance that he can get to you unharmed. So order him to stay where he is. Tell him that you will have to protect yourself if he moves. The important thing here is that his dangerous intentions, and your understanding of them as such, should also be clear to any bystander. If you are being threatened by an unarmed five year old kid… Well, this is what a disparate force standard is all about. The verbal threat has to be coming from someone who has adequate force to diminish your ability to resist even more physical abuse which, as it accumulates, endangers your health and then your life. But consider this; one slap in the face can lead to this downward spiral even when the person slapping you is smaller. If you have given him the chance to reduce your superior force, as George Zimmerman did with Trayvon Martin (Google "Trayvon Martin Case") you have a whole new situation to assess. At this point, someone half your size has become capable of doing you serious harm because you let him get the first punch in, or otherwise could not avoid it.

Serious harm is any harm that could so diminish your capacity to defend yourself that even more serious harm could come to you. Think of all the harm that can diminish your capacity to defend yourself. One good sock in the face could leave you helpless to prevent more of them even if it does not cause more than tissue damage (bruising) and a headache. Just the shock of it is disabling. People know this. The attacker knows this. Once he has you down you have waited too long, you have accepted too much risk.

If the assailant has a gun being pointed at the floor, and he is not in motion, you may choose to proceed with taking control of the legal structure of the situation by your verbal and bodily behavior. This is where your training in managing more risk than you might otherwise have to, if the reasonableness standard were actually precise, comes into play. If it is too late for this, you will have to let the situation speak for itself. You are not obligated to suffer any harm which could diminish your capacity to save yourself without deadly force, even when you are bigger and stronger.

CHAPTER 4

DEPLOYING THE GUN

It is time to repeat our disclaimer. You must make yourself familiar with the laws in your own state with respect to self-defense with deadly force. Nothing we are describing below is a guarantee that you will be behaving legally in your own state, or that a prosecutor is not going to succeed in convicting you in any event. Carrying a gun and finally using it in self-defense has inherent, inbuilt risk. When you decide to accept that risk you are deciding that it is better to be alive *with* the legal problems, than dead without them.

> ***"We think these responses are ethical and effective. We cannot guarantee that they are legal in your state."***

What we describe below is what we would do. It is a partial inventory of logically and contingently possible reactions to a threatening situation. We think these responses are *ethical and effective.* We cannot guarantee that they are *legal* in your state.

For example, you are being verbally threatened by a potential assailant who has a gun in hand even though it is not pointed at you – yet. He has deployed a weapon, it is in his hand, and he is telling you he intends to harm you. Even if he puts conditions on this, there is no guarantee that he is not about to aim and shoot. If you were in a store where a man was threatening anyone else, especially a member of your own family, with a gun in his hand but not as yet pointed, would you hesitate to shoot? The standard here is what you would want, and even expect, someone else to do for you. When someone is holding a gun in his hand, and threatening you, both the ethical and effective reaction is to shoot – now.

In other situations of serious but less immediate threat, for example where the distance between you and the aggressor is substantial and the nature of the

> ***"Brandishing is part of controlling the situation and characterizing it for others."***

aggressor's weapon means he is not able to harm you at a moment's notice, you must start making the nature of the situation clear to others with your verbal and bodily behavior. Again, your message to the bystanders is that you or someone else is in serious danger. This message could include brandishing your gun.

In thousands of situations each year in America, brandishing a gun defensively ends the situation with no harm coming to anyone. Exactly what you will do is a judgment call where each version of brandishing your gun may be a stronger response to a more intense situation. Brandishing is part of controlling the situation and characterizing it for others. It is a sign of your fear that you or someone else is in danger of being harmed or killed, but also a sign that you will not be a victim, that you are not going to be controlled by the situation.

You might simply unconceal the gun. You might grip the gun while keeping it in its holster, but in this case it better be clear to the aggressor that you are actually gripping a gun. If this is not enough to cause the aggressor to cease and desist or give you enough time to withdraw, then the next level of brandishing is to draw the gun and not point it. At this point you must still be beyond his reach.

The last step is to ready the gun while you are still calm enough to make sure that you are gripping it properly over a stable stance. At this point you are making it clear that you are ready to shoot. You are aiming.

GRIPPING THE GUN

There is now a truly professional body of knowledge about how to grip a handgun with a view to turning your hands, arms, and torso into what it should be – a solid platform for actually aiming, and not just pointing, the gun, and managing recoil so the gun returns to its original aimed position instantly.

This proper grip does not feel natural for most people – at first. But we can promise you it will become very natural in the long run precisely because your brain will associate the correct grip with control of the weapon. And that is what your brain is looking for as you deploy the weapon.

This ideal grip is a two-handed affair which extends control of the gun up into the backward direction of recoil, so the recoil is not acting on a low fulcrum (imagine what would happen if you discharged your weapon while holding it at the very bottom of the grip). You cannot put your hands directly behind the slide. This much should be obvious. (We have seen people put their thumbs on the back of the slide, which leads to disaster.) But the higher your hands are on the grip, that is, the closer they are to the level of the recoil, the more your grip is managing the recoil straight-forwardly.

Get your grip as high into the beaver tail as possible. This is basic to recoil management.

The possibility of this grip is a real advantage to semi-automatic pistols versus revolvers, where the grip of the revolver is much lower than the plane of the recoil. Again, imagine the gun being flipped out of your hand backwards as it goes off, due to your grip being too far below the barrel.

The higher up you can get your dominant hand on the grip of the gun, the better. If you are afraid that the slide of the gun is going to slice across the fleshy area in between your thumb and index finger then buy a pistol with a beaver tail which will lay over and protect this area, or fit a beaver tail to a pistol which does not start out with one. There are plenty of aftermarket beaver tails that a gunsmith can install for you, or which you can install yourself (although ensure you are not adding features to your pistol that may cause it to snag on clothing in the draw).

As you grip the gun with your dominant hand, high up toward the slide, your thumb and index finger should be pointed straight toward the target. You will put the tip or middle of the end section of the index finger on the trigger when you are ready to shoot. Do not wrap the first knuckle of your trigger finger around the trigger. This will result in pushing the barrel left on average if you are right handed, and vice versa. In order to push the trigger straight backward, so the aim stays right on target, you will need to use the area between the first knuckle and the end of your finger for discharging the weapon.

Now take your non-dominant hand and push the base of it against the base of your dominant hand, which is already gripping the gun. Put its thumb, underneath the thumb of the dominant hand. Three fingers should now be pointing directly at your target. The thumb and index finger of your dominant hand are pointing from two different sides of the weapon. The thumb of your non-dominant hand is under the thumb of your dominant hand, and it is also pointing at your target. Wrap the fingers of your non-dominant hand around the outside of the fingers of your dominant hand.

Now place the thumb of your non-dominant hand far forward either on the slide of the gun, or just under it. Many pistols have a place which is stippled where you can place the end of this non-dominant thumb just below the slide. Do not worry about placing it on the slide. It will not hurt you as it actuates. You will not even notice it sliding across the print of your thumb.

When you are done properly gripping your gun, your two thumbs should be pointing at the target on one side, and your index finger should be pointing at the target on the other side.

As you move the gun out to aim it, locking your elbows, your hands should close in on the gun like a nutcracker, increasing the compression of your grip. But don't try to hold the gun in an extremely tight way. It should come naturally with this levering compression as you push the weapon out to aim it at eye level. If you are too tight, too rigid, you may actually set up a little shaking in your arms and shoulders which will degrade your aim.

At this point your grip is giving you tremendous control over the left and right pointing angle of the weapon, as well as the barrel's movement up and down. It will feel strange at first to have your hands, especially your non-dominant hand, moved out so far toward the front of the gun. But it is basic physics. The farther out along the barrel of the gun that your non-dominant hand rests – mainly the thumb – the easier it is to steady the windage of the weapon, its movement left and right. Remember, your hands, your body, is just a platform for the gun. It must be a steady platform.

Your arms are forming a sharp triangle which meets at your hands, compressing the gun like a couple of levers. With our elbows locked and your body leaning just slightly forward to manage the recoil, you have become a stable platform for the weapon. If you do not keep your weight slightly forward, the recoil will push you back on your heels. You will have to recover your balance before you can aim again.

Grip the gun tightly by levering your palms against the grip with your forearms.

Once you have achieved the proper grip with your weight slightly forward, you can fine tune your aim by lining up the front and back sights, and making sure the top of the front sight is level with the top of the back sight. With practice, you will be surprised at how fast you can achieve this deadly aiming position, and put the sights on target.

You do not have to lean over the gun, with rounded shoulders and your eyes up in their sockets. Stretch up and get the slide the gun level with your eyes. If you have your head and neck down too far you will be uncomfortable. Your eyes will be rolling up in their sockets and you will not have a full view of the scene in front of you. You should learn to shoot with both eyes open.

Over and over again, we have seen people who could not even get on paper at a shooting range, start shooting in a deadly fashion after being taught this now orthodox, standard two-handed grip. Nothing else will increase your accuracy so exponentially as this well-studied, well established method. We might even refer to it as the 'professional grip.'

Older grips, such as resting your dominant hand, the one gripping the gun, on the palm of your non-dominant hand are, to put it bluntly, pure nonsense. This is essentially just a one handed grip.

There is a time and place in combat shooting for a one handed grip, for shooting on your back, or side, or on the run, and ad infinitum. But the grip we have described here is what you should train yourself to achieve within a second of pulling your pistol from its holster. If you make this grip automatic so you can actually aim the gun, you will be ready to actually shoot the threat instead of everything around him, and be done in one or two shots. It's all about neutralizing the threat as fast as you can, and really aiming is essential to this. Even old west gunfighters often won by letting the opponent fire in a panic while *he* took the time to aim.

"It's all about neutralizing the threat as fast as you can, and really aiming is essential to this."

With your weight slightly forward, your body will absorb recoil without being pushed off balance on your heels. Your body and your arms will return automatically to the pre-shot position, on target.

YOUR DOMINANT EYE

If you do not have a dominant eye, you have a challenge in front of you. For shooting, you will have to train your brain to use one eye or the other as if it is dominant, while keeping both eyes open. This can be done. This process may require some professional advice and help. The last resort is to habitually aim with one eye closed. In combat, this is a serious disadvantage.

Most people have a dominant eye and can quickly determine which one it is. Hopefully, your dominant eye lines up with your dominant hand. If it does not, you will have to train yourself to shoot with your non-dominant hand, or train your eyes, once again, to cooperate with the dominant hand at least while you are shooting. Again, you should contact a local trainer about this challenge. There is almost always a solution.

To determine which eye is dominant if you do not already know, stretch out the arm of your dominant hand with your thumb up. Now, with both eyes open, cover some object in your field of vision with your thumb. Now close one eye. If the thumb moves then the eye you closed is dominant. If the thumb stays where it is, then the eye you closed is non-dominant.

This should show you that with both eyes open, your dominant eye will keep you on target when aiming. In most people the dominant eye lines up with the dominant hand, and this makes proceeding with your training much easier than when there is a conflict between your dominant eye and dominant hand, or no clear dominant eye. Grip the gun with your dominant hand. This will line it up with your dominant eye, and you are in business, with both eyes open.

PRESBYOPIA

If you are older, you may have presbyopia. The tiny muscles your eye uses to bend and focus the lens of your eye are no longer up to the job. You need reading glasses or bifocals to keep things in focus within a foot or two of the lens of your eye. The problem may be severe enough that you cannot keep the sights of a pistol in focus. The background, the target, in the meantime, may be in perfect focus.

There are solutions to this problem. Each comes with a challenge.

Shooting with reading glasses on, keeping the sights in focus, and lined up, with the background target appearing a bit fuzzy, can be the very best solution. In combat you are shooting for center mass. It does not matter if the target is a bit fuzzy as long as it is within pistol range. We have seen people shoot very accurately at the center of fuzzy targets down range, with the sights in perfect focus and lined up to center mass. We believe in the primacy of keeping the iron sights in focus.

But there is another, albeit more expensive, solution. Dot sights, getting their energy either from the sun (fiber optic sights) or a battery (electronic sights) exist on a single plane and are easy to keep in focus without reading glasses, while the background is still in focus with both eyes open (to be clear: by "dot sight" we mean the type, also known as a "reflex" sight, that reflect a dot onto a semireflective glass-like material, through which you look and obtain your sight picture, not laser sights that project a dot of light onto the actual target). With a dot sight there is no lining up of a back sight and a front sight. There is less temptation to close your non-dominant eye which reduces your peripheral vision by half. In combat, keeping both eyes open is important. It is another detail that can save your life.

Dot sights are keeping older people shooting very effectively. Once the dot is sighted in, it will stay on target no matter what angle you see it from through the back window of the sight. If the dot is on target, the gun is on target. This can be a huge advantage in combat – as long as you can quickly find the dot.

And this is the problem with the dot sight solution. Dot sights on handguns are small. You have a small window in which to find the dot. Your eye still has to be lined up correctly with the sight to see the dot. There is such a long distance between your eyes and the sight, when your arms are correctly outstretched, that the dot is easily covered by the angle of the gun (and therefore the sides of the electronic sight). The sight is like a straight, virtual tunnel, which you have to be looking straight through to see the dot at the end of the tunnel. Even when the dot is bright enough to stand up to daylight, if you do not learn to bring the gun up consistently to the same place, where the dot is not hidden by the angle of the gun, you will end up searching for it by twisting and turning the gun until it appears.

As the technology improves this challenge may be mitigated. If you have the time to train with a dot sight, you may overcome the problem reliably enough to keep a dot sight on your carry gun. Just remember that it is better to be able to find your front and back sight *now*, even when the background might be somewhat fuzzy, than have to look for a dot while the assailant is shooting. Most gun fights occur in very close quarters. Picking up the target in the background is not the challenge. Getting on target, even a fuzzy target, by lining up your sights and striking first, is the goal.

So which is more challenging? Finding a dot sight quickly, or making sure that you have reading glasses on when you end up in a gun fight, so you can line up the iron sights very quickly? (In other words, you can't just leave your reading glasses in the car.) It is your call. If you do not buy a dot sight, and you have presbyopia, then you should train yourself to shoot with and without your reading glasses. Without your reading glasses, the target will be sharp and your sights will be fuzzy. You must still try to get those sights lined up. You may find that you shoot just as well without your reading glasses as you do with them. Somehow, the sharpness of the target is making up for the fuzziness of the sights. But there's no guarantee of this. You will have to figure out how it is working for you.

There are 'peep' style back sights for handguns. Although theoretically these might help with presbyopia, we have not been impressed by them. With the front sight being fuzzy up and down vertically, it is still difficult for people, without reading glasses, to center the front post fuzz in the back circular fuzz. But then all we are saying is that peep sights, in our experience, do not seem to be any better than standard iron sights for people with this problem. We cannot say they are worse.

AIMING THE GUN

To end the threat quickly, you have to aim. Otherwise you are just relying on luck.

In the past, even the recent past, some 'experts' have tried to advance a theory and a practice based on the premise that because a handgun fight is so stressful and usually occurs in close quarters, it is best to just instinctively point, not aim, your gun. As far as we know, based on this approach, police officers have accumulated a lot of experience completely missing their targets. One of the primary reasons why training is so highly motivated for anyone serious about self-defense is that aiming is essential, and this means you have to train to the point of unholstering and aiming automatically. If you have to think about it, you will be slowed down. If you do not aim, you may become the victim or it may take much more time than it should to deal with the situation. The longer it drags on, the more dangerous and damaging it becomes.

With practice, aiming becomes easy; it becomes automatic. Under stress your muscle memory will do what it has been trained to do, what is drilled into it. This can save your life.

Aiming means that your iron sights are in alignment, with the front post in between the uprights of the back notch. It also means that the top of the front post is level with the top of the uprights of the back notch.

Correct iron sight picture.

This is often referred to as the weapon being 'trained' but not necessarily on target. Your goal is to quickly 'train' your weapon, and then get it on target. You can easily do both at the same time if your target is not moving. With enough training of your body and mind, you can do both at the same time even while your target is moving. The human brain has an amazing capacity to calculate where a moving object is going to be next. If this were not the case wide receivers would not be catching the football as often as they do and the guy in the left field of a baseball diamond would not be picking off line drives. Theoretically, if you are as adept with your handgun as you can become with a baseball glove, your brain will tell you where to aim at a moving target. If we can do this with shotguns (and remember how well Annie Oakley did it with *rifles*) then, in principle, we can do it with a handgun. In close combat our target is much bigger than a clay pigeon.

Getting the front posts and back posts lined up, side to side, and up and down, is how the handgun is calibrated, or 'trained', as a platform for delivering the bullet to the right location. It means that both your windage and elevation are now clear. The next step is to get the target into the sight picture as quickly as you can. You are on target when the front and back sights are correctly aligned (your gun is trained) and the targeted location is in view right behind the front post.

In a gun fight, you are aiming for the center of the body mass. Adjusting your aim up to the chest cavity is ideal. Keep in mind that if you hit an assailant right where the neck meets the chest, dead center (the dimple in between the collar bones), the bullet will sever the spine and the perp will drop instantly. He will not have the time or ability to pull his trigger on the way down. Obviously this is a specialized shot to be used only under the appropriate circumstances. It is motivated in a situation where the assailant is not in motion and has to be incapacitated instantly because of what he can otherwise do – like setting off a bomb. It is a SWAT team shot. Nevertheless understanding the biology of this shot might, under some rare circumstance, become useful.

"It has to be held tightly, but not much more than a firm grip asserts automatically."

Once the gun is up, and your arms are locked into a triangle, your hands will compress on the gun to just about the right degree automatically. As we have already discussed, if you grip even harder you may induce some tremor. It has to be held tightly, but not much more than a firm grip asserts automatically as you push your arms out in front of you while gripping the gun properly.

Now think of your body, from the waist down, as a platform with the gun mounted on it, something like the way we mount rotating guns on the deck of a ship. Your upper body is the gun compartment in which the gun proper is rigidly installed. It is the gun compartment which moves left and right, while the gun proper aims up and down. In your case the gun compartment – what the gun is directly attached to (your upper body) – pivots due to the twisting of your torso in one direction or the other. Your arms are outstretched and locked into position. The handgun is trained. From the waist up you can rotate left and right, your feet firmly planted, your body listing forward just slightly to counter balance the recoil which will travel straight back through your rigid arms. Rotate your upper torso to bring your gun to its target. This is a smooth and very stable motion. It is an ideal motion and not always possible in a gun fight. But strive for it.

As soon as you have turned your arms and torso into a weight forward platform for your gun, you can leave your feet planted and rotate at the waist to cover almost 180 degrees of target motion.

Competitive shooting is the best way to make this way of controlling your gun reflexive. Competitive shooters learn to "prep" their trigger (prepare it for discharge, meaning it is pulled straight back just to the point where it is ready to break) as they move from one target to another in a shooting 'stage' by moving their whole upper body. The feet stay planted. The trigger is at a hair when the center of the target comes into view as the shooter follows the front sight with his eyes. This prevents flinching – pulling or pushing the gun off target as it discharges. His peripheral vision is helping him predict exactly when to break the trigger. A good shooter may keep moving right through several targets this way without altering the speed or direction of his upper body swing. It starts in the torso, not in the shoulders or arms. Your shoulders and arms are part of the rigid compartment that your handgun is installed in.

If you want to improve rapidly, join a competitive shooting league. There are plenty of divisions for beginners and you can use a wide variety of handguns.

If you are using a dot sight, perhaps because you have the presbyopia we have already discussed, your first challenge is finding the dot. As mentioned earlier, this will be a matter of practice. Once the dot is in view and it is placed over your target it is just a matter of discharging the firearm without flinching. The dot sight supports a liberal level of discipline in your grip and the position of your body as a platform for the gun. But all of the rules for aiming with iron sights still apply. The main difference is that you will not be trying to line up a back sight and front sight existing on two different planes. This can speed up training your gun and then searching for the target. It is a mistake to think that your gun no longer needs to be aligned. In order to hit the target it always has to be aligned. What the dot sight is designed to make easier and faster is this alignment. By simply placing the dot over the target your gun is both trained and aimed.

Now the only question is whether your grip and stance are good for suppressing flinch, and for managing the recoil. Since you still have to aim and manage recoil, all of the same biomechanical discipline applies.

On the other hand, as a gunfight degrades into a situation where your body positions may include being on your back, laying on your belly, laying on your side, crouching, reaching over cover and so on, the value of the dot sight increases. You just have to concentrate on the dot and then the background sight picture with both eyes open. There is plenty of eye relief[1] because you do not have to try to keep both a front and back sight in focus, as well as the whole sight picture. If you

1. "Eye Relief" refers to the distance between your eye and your pistol's optic. Consider a telescope: you can use it effectively only when your eye is very close to its eyepiece lens; it therefore offers low eye relief. In defensive combat, greater eye relief provides the ability to acquire a target more rapidly, and enables greater situational awareness.

can easily find your dot sight under pressure in a gun fight, then it may just be the best option whether or not you suffer from presbyopia.

MORE ON SIGHTS

The sights you choose to install on your gun are extremely important. They have to work for you. They could save your life.

Aperture sights, with two posts in back and a single post in front, do not disappear in bright sunlight. The brighter the better for aperture sights. In bright light the rear sight, the front sight, and the target all snap into focus. But at night, black iron sights can be almost impossible to use. This is why many iron sites these days are coated with a luminous treatment or paint, or have luminous dots on the posts of the rear sight and the post of the front sight facing toward the back.

Compared to both black iron sights and iron sights enhanced with luminescence, the electronic dot sight shines, literally, at night as well as during the day. Everything else may be covered in darkness, but you can always see your sight. You still know where the bullet is going to go in your whole field of view.

Like the dot sight, you can always see a laser sight at night. A laser sight shoots a concentrated beam of light out from the frame of the sight attached to your gun. Like the dot sight it is usually red or green. This beam lands on the target and is pointing to where your bullet will go assuming the sight has been accurately aligned with the barrel – 'sighted in'. All of these sight types can be adjusted, usually using allen wrenches, to make sure that they indicate where the bullet will end up at the yardage for which it was fine-tuned.

Contemporary pistols are quite accurate when you do not flinch. And most of them can be counted on to deliver the bullet almost exactly where you are pointing. When you see people at the range struggling with a handgun to just get the bullet on paper, let alone anywhere near the bullseye, we can assure you the problem is the shooter, not the gun, ninety-nine percent of the time. These very same people will find that with the proper grip, stance, and trigger pull (drawing the trigger straight back) their accuracy will increase exponentially.

Unlike the dot sight you cannot always see the laser sight during the day. In bright light the laser beam gets washed out to the point of invisibility. It may help to make the laser blink, and many laser sights come with this option. They typically have three settings. Off, on, without blinking and on, with blinking. In our experience, with or without blinking, laser sights are almost impossible to find in daylight outside. In that case you will have to use your iron sights. (We have never seen a gun which comes with a laser sight which does not also come with iron sights.) Laser sights are a good option for inside shooting during the day and night. They are a good option for nighttime shooting just about anywhere.

When we consider the speed of training and aiming a gun and visibility in different levels of light, the electronic dot sight, if you can learn to use it – to acquire the dot instantly as you draw your gun – beats the other sight options, whether you have presbyopia or not. It may be the very best option for people who are put off by the challenge of aligning iron sights under pressure. The electronic dot sight is visible during the day because it shines inside of its own frame instead of invading the outside light like a laser. It is also perfectly visible to the gun handler at night, just like the laser sight. If you get comfortable, that is fast, with an electronic dot sight, the only disadvantages we can think of is the battery running low at the wrong time and place and the fact that it is less intimidating to a targeted aggressor at night, who may very well withdraw the moment he sees a laser sight reflected off of his own body. (Aim the laser at his chest, not his head, so he can see it). One of the disciplines required of your commitment to a dot sight, is to make sure you have a fully charged battery in the sight when you carry it.

A dot sight enables you not only to focus on your target but to acquire secondary threat targets more effectively.

CHAPTER 5

ENDING THE THREAT

Having deployed and aimed your gun quickly and accurately, shoot to kill. Aim for center mass. The idea of shooting to wound, once the assailant has behaved in a fashion which justifies deadly force in the first place, is the wrong idea. It is designed to make you feel better about what you are doing. It is self-indulgent. If you fail, because you are not being decisive and accepting the situation for what it is, you will feel worse afterward in case you are still alive. (What if you are crippled?) There is nothing moral and therefore rational about *correctly* deciding that deadly force is required, and then failing to use it or using it in a fashion which is more dangerous for bystanders than it is for the criminal attacking you, or them. You can easily see for yourself that an attempt at fancy shooting under such overwhelming stress is much more likely to harm a bystander than aiming for center mass on the perpetrator. What if, in trying to wound the assailant, you wound or kill a bystander? This could happen in any event if you are not using personal protection rounds which stop inside of the assailant. (Many very good quasi-frangible concealed carry rounds are available these days in most handgun calibers. Buy them and use them for concealed carry. Do not carry full metal jacket practice rounds which will travel through your target into someone else.) Do not make things worse by shooting any kind of round at the periphery of the assailant's profile.

> ***"Your job is to do what you set out to do when you drew your gun and aimed it – eliminate the threat to yourself and others."***

Your job is to do what you set out to do when you drew your gun *and aimed it* – eliminate the threat to yourself and others. In shooting to kill it is likely that you will wound your attacker to the point where he is disabled. If you shoot to wound, you may not disable him at all. Before God and man, when the situation justifies deadly force, that is exactly what you should use in order to succeed to the degree required. You will find this is easier when someone invades your home or is otherwise threatening your spouse or child. If you are protecting someone else remember that they are someone else's spouse or child.

> **"Combat, constrained by law and morality, can be complicated."**

What is required is to eliminate the threat as fast as you can – and then stop. It is certainly eliminated when the perp is dead. But the key legal point, here at the end of the self-defense process and the beginning of the legal process, is to stop abruptly, when the threat has ended. The attacker may or may not be dead. As long as he is incapable of any further threat, you must keep your wits about you and stop shooting. If you empty your gun into a man who is already down, you will have legal problems. On the other hand, as long as he is pointing a gun at you, even if he is on his back, the threat has not yet been eliminated. If he is down with a knife, and incapable of reaching you with it, the fight is over.

So you have to balance two principles:
(1) Shoot to kill when deadly force is justified in the first place.
(2) Stop shooting, in any event, as soon as the threat is eliminated.

Obviously the second principle applies whether or not there are witnesses and whether or not you might get sued by the survivor. It is what you have to do morally and legally.

If you were obligated by law to shoot to wound, our right to carry would not be the inhibition to crime we want it to be. The law is on your side if deadly force is justified in the first place, and you stop the instant the threat is eliminated.

No one is denying that this is a judgment call. When someone is struggling to raise his gun one more time to shoot you, the judgment is still clear. The danger is clear and present. But things can obviously get complicated. A man who is still angry, profane, and has the gun in his hand, seemingly without the strength to raise it, is on the border. Combat, constrained by law and morality, can be complicated. If you are still sincerely in fear of death or injury, you may still be shooting at this point. But if your judgment tells you that it is over, just cover yourself. Be ready. What you have to be able to testify to honestly is that you were still in fear for your life during the last break of your trigger.

CHAPTER 6

AFTER ACTIONS

After the threat has been eliminated, return your gun to its concealed carry position on your body. Do not lay it on the ground or put it on some counter, or give it to someone else. Keep control of the gun. Make sure it is reconcealed so it does not trigger the blood pressure and defensive reactions of a police officer arriving on the scene.

> **"If at all possible, leave first aid to someone else."**

Do not leave the scene. Make a note of where the assailant's weapon is. Do not let anyone touch it. Obviously you want the police to see that weapon and photograph it on or near the body of the assailant. Move the weapon only to disarm a surviving attacker. Try to do so in a manner which does not obscure the aggressor's finger prints.

Call an ambulance, even you think your assailant is dead. Then make sure that you or someone else calls the police. Almost everywhere in the United States today it is all the same phone number – 911.

Do not alter any aspect of the scene.

If at all possible, leave first aid to someone else. If you are alone with the wounded aggressor, you may decide to apply first aid. You should not do so if this just puts you back in any danger (do not put yourself in a position where a wounded perp could grab your gun). You should also consider that you may later rely in court on forensic evidence and should as far as possible preserve the crime scene. It is your judgment call. Any rational district attorney is going to conclude that you have nothing to hide about the nature of your actions when you try to save the life of the attacker.

When the police arrive have your hands in the air, away from your body, away from the holster. Tell them where the gun is and the police will take it away from you without you having to touch it. They will probably cuff you first. Get ready for being treated as if you are the criminal. Knowing this is going to happen before it happens will keep you calm.

Keep your conversation with the police simple, factual, and limited. You, or someone else, was being attacked, or was under threat, and you behaved defensively. If the assailant is still alive tell the police that you want to press charges. After keeping things this simple, tell them that you want to call your lawyer and that you require him to be present in the face of any more questioning. Your goal is to avoid irritating the police by providing them with some basic information, while avoiding any accidental, tragic choice of words which could lead them to suspect that you have violated the principles of legitimate self-defense. If the police have cuffed you, you are under arrest and your legal defense has begun.

You should have a card in your purse or wallet with the phone number of your concealed carry insurance company. There are several to choose from today. They all issue subscribers a card with a twenty-four hour hotline on it. You will call this number to report the incident and get a lawyer active on your case immediately. You can find contact information for the insurance carriers on the internet.

- United States Concealed Carry Association (USCCA)
- Armed Citizens Legal Defense Network (ACLDN)
- U.S. Law Shield
- NRA Carry Guard

"The police are not your enemy. But neither are they your friend."

If you know you have enough time before the police arrive, call your provider before they get there. Otherwise, be ready to put your hands in the air and deal safely with this first contact with the police.

Some experts will recommend that you not say a word to the police without your lawyer present. This doctrine is based on the theory that the police are always willing to twist something you say into full blown suspicion and prosecution. If you lack confidence in your ability to keep your conversation disciplined enough, or if you simply decide, at the time, that you are too nervous to consciously manage what you say, you might very politely tell that police that stress is making any conversation impossible until your attorney is present. Ask the police only where they are taking you and pass the information through to your attorney or the representative on the phone. Obviously, whenever you are carrying your gun you should be carrying your phone.

Above all else do not lecture the police about the law or what happened. Do not attempt to try the case right then and there. All the 'facts' will come out. This can start when your attorney is present.

Insofar as you are a law-abiding citizen, the police are not your enemy. But neither are they your friend. They are an arm of the government. And the government is not there to exonerate you.

PART 4

THE LAW AND SELF-DEFENSE

CHAPTER 1

THE LAW AND 'RATIONALLY' JUSTIFIED LETHAL FORCE

In Appendix A we have provided links to information about statutes which describe lawful and unlawful standards of self-defense, specific to each state. Here, we address the all-compassing and universal standard of 'rationality' for your actions. Every state is going to hold you accountable for behaving 'unreasonably' as you defend yourself or another. But what does it mean to behave reasonably or unreasonably? Just how objective could this standard possibly be if the laws do not break this standard down into more specific, measurable criteria for actual behavior? The message we provide here, at a national level, is that you will have to strive for the highest standard of 'rationality' which you can conceive of, especially as you travel across state lines with your gun, while not being an expert on the laws of each and every jurisdiction. This in turn, becomes a tactical issue. To ensure living up to a standard of 'rationality' that just about any jury or judge can respect, *you must be tactically capable of managing more risk* than you would otherwise have to manage if the standards were both clear and modest. There is a profound

"The rationality standard is not clear and not objective, despite what you may have been told."

difference between a standard of 'rationality' as such and a standard, a measure, of concrete, historical behavior. And this is the problem. The rationality standard is not clear and not objective, despite what you may have been told. It can't be.

No matter what state you live in, the heart of your legal defense for using deadly force is all about satisfying a standard of rational justification. But then what is *the* standard of rationality, of the 'reasonableness' of using deadly force? What does it mean to make your decision to use deadly force *objectively* 'rational'? In one concealed carry expert's book we read:

The key word is "reasonable," which is an external, *objective* standard… In the legal context, whether or not something is "reasonable" isn't a matter of opinion; it's a matter of fact. Matters of fact are determined by a trier of fact – usually a jury…"

"Under analysis, facts just turn out to be judgments which the judge or jury asserts are true."

Unfortunately, this is an incoherent statement. It is simply wrong, philosophically. On the one hand the writer asserts that the reasonableness of your actions is a matter of fact. On the other hand he reminds us that whether or not your actions are reasonable will be decided by the jury. But if the rationality of your actions is really a fact, one way or another, it should not be a decision, a judgment call, that the jury makes.

Under analysis, facts just turn out to be judgments which the judge or jury asserts are true. The person making the judgment *chooses* the language with which to state the fact. This language does not select itself. It might be relative. Standards of rationality are not themselves facts, they are relative measures.

On the one hand the passage quoted above asserts the objectivity and, by implication, the universality of the rational standard, but then asserts that this standard is something which the jury *decides.* Apparently, the standard is not an explicit measure given to us in the law which is somehow clearly applicable to the action. The action in question almost always involves, legally, the complexity of one's state of mind – one's fear of death or great bodily harm whether or not this fear was objectively 'true', or 'valid', or 'rational' (choose your term).

Because the rationality standard is actually just a judgment made by a jury or a judge, and cannot be anything else, it explains exactly why it is so legally risky to use deadly force. If there were really an objective, universal, factual standard of rationality (transcendent of tradition, culture, language, juries, *human judgment*), there would be much less risk. We would not need a jury, or judge, to decide. The police could decide the matter all the time, making the trial process totally unnecessary. The standard would, in some mysterious way, be out there, objectively. It would be like a ruler floating over everyone's head – a special, objective ruler with which action can be measured for its 'reasonableness'. Clearly this judgment is not like judging whether your bodily movements are fast or slow or whether you have jumped five feet or six feet. The rationality standard is metaphysical, not behavioristic.

In finally admitting that juries *decide* what the facts are we are admitting that 'facts', including what is reasonable and what is not, are actually just democratic judgments.

From a philosophical *and practical* point of view, this notion that the jury's or judge's rationality is 'objective' and 'not a matter of opinion' is pure nonsense. This bold claim that there is an 'objective' standard of what is reasonable (so we can identify reasonable conclusions, reasonable arguments, and reasonable behavior) is immediately and ironically juxtaposed in our legal system with the commitment *to let the jury decide.* Why would we have to use this method if the standard is objective and universal? A jury is a temporary, highly limited, and relative device for *deciding* the truth. And this is precisely why both defense attorneys and prosecutors hire psychologists to help them manipulate juries.

So setting aside this pretense about the objectivity, and therefore the universality, of the rational standard, the truly practical advice is to imagine how a jury, in your case, in your state, in your subculture – a jury of your peers – would react to your decision to use deadly force. Whether legal experts like it or not, or know how to exploit it or not, this might be relative. It might be very demonstrably relative to which gender is on trial. It might be demonstrably relative to a culture or a subculture. These days we even have juries which 'nullify' the law. This is, in effect, a democratic decision to reform the law.

"You are at the mercy of a particular police department, prosecutor, jury and judge."

So instead of imagining that there is some objective, scientific standard of rationality which you can latch onto, which transcends the judgment of a jury let alone a judge or police officer, recognize that you are taking on the risk that a jury will *not* see it your way. The jury may not actually be made up of your peers.

In effect, we are arguing that experts who tell you that rationality is an 'objective' standard, are actually falsifying (mistakenly diminishing) your risk. (Can you describe this standard operationally? Can your neighbor?) When we tell you there is no such 'objective', universal standard, we are the ones who are actually forcing you to see just how risky your use of deadly force can be. You are at the mercy of a particular police department, prosecutor, jury and judge. This is the agreed upon and extremely modest sense in which the standard is externalized.

"Think carefully about whether or not a jury can identify with <u>your</u> judgment."

The reasonableness standard is just democratic. It has been confusing for hundreds of years for the 'experts' to suggest that this also means it is objective or universal. It is, they finally admit, the property of your community, the property of a jury. It is external only in this sense. The text of the law says that the standard is, itself, rationality. Obviously, this is a very abstract 'standard.' The statutes do not tell us what objective, universal rationality is – they do not do technical philosophy. Neither does the jury. It makes its *judgment*, in context. Think carefully about whether or not a jury can identify with *your* judgment. Some juries may think it is reasonable for a woman who is being stalked to buy a gun, stalk the stalker, and kill him. But assuming this is extremely risky. Way too risky. You have to manage the risk. No one else, not your lawyer, or judge, or jury, can do this for you as you engage in self-defense.

The law says you cannot be the aggressor when you use deadly force. But then who is the aggressor, the male stalker, or the female who refuses to be victimized? What are the 'facts' here?

We do not help concealed carry permit holders by offering them superficial platitudes about these utterly vague legal standards. The useful point is more adult.

You must be very, very conservative in using deadly force. Unfortunately, any given jury in your community may require you, in order to be acquitted, to put yourself in more danger than you think is at all reasonable.

In fact, this is a common bias within the law and order community as such. The whole point of acquiring a permit and a gun is to lessen your risk. We are here to tell you that the heart of the matter is that the legal system is, in effect, forcing you to accept a lot of tactical risk before you pull the trigger. It is ironic but true. A woman who is being stalked by a very threatening man has, on average, to take on the risk of not initiating an aggressive defense.

The practical implication of the ambiguity of the rationality standard, is that *you must be trained to take on tactical risk while not threatening your well-being*. The ambiguity, the contingency of the trial process, forces you to accept tactical risk *if you wish to achieve a high level of confidence in the outcome.* If you are forced (perhaps by virtue of living in a liberal city) to take on a lot of tactical risk as part of keeping your own rational standard very demanding, you need training. You have to manage the risk *under stress.*

Imagine a society in the future in which, on average, juries allow women to respond very aggressively to a stalker. The juries, in a culturally relative fashion, consistently consider an aggressive response (perhaps engaging the stalker through a window, before he has actually entered the residence with a visible weapon or after a verbal threat even without a visible weapon) a form of reasonable self-defense. Tactically, for the woman, this situation is much simpler than the other situation where she is expected to wait until she is actually attacked inside of her residence. In this latter case tactical training is quite literally implied by the *lack* of a specified objective rational standard (the universal problem which will never go away) and the lack of any clear *tradition*.

One of the practical implications of this discussion is carefully considering whether or not you want to be tried by a judge or a jury. Be careful. Your lawyer might think that trying you before a judge is more profitable, when what you need is a jury that can identify with you. A good lawyer will help you decide whose standard of rationality is more like your own – the judge's or the jury's.

The 'rationality' standard for assessing your behavior during a defensive act of violence goes across everything you do. Again, it is the all-encompassing legal standard.

Local concealed carry trainers should have more information about the rationality standard in those of your state's statutes which circumscribe self-defense. But wherever the stated standard is itself "reasonableness" rather than specific standards of rationality, you can only consider examples of behavioral standards that have and have not passed muster at trial. We believe there is a central tendency, a pattern of behavior which people universally consider reasonable uses of deadly force. But we also believe that the edges of this bell curve of behavior are fuzzy enough to recommend training – the training that helps you to manage the tactical risk which is implied by using deadly force only when you really have to. Your local trainers will often be knowledgeable enough to provide scenario-based training and even refer you to case law where the scenarios were recognized as legal and illegal.

PART 5

HOME DEFENSE

CHAPTER 1

INTRODUCTION TO HOME DEFENSE

Depending upon where you live, it may be more likely that your home will be invaded than that you will ever face a life-threatening situation outside of your home.

Most states, for quite some time now, do not require you to retreat from your own home when threatened by an invader. Outside of your home you are usually required to retreat if you can, unless your state has a sprawling 'castle doctrine' which increases the boundaries of your castle, making it wherever you are. Otherwise, your home is clearly your castle and you have the right to defend your life within it without retreating. But the standards for using deadly force still apply. You have to feel threatened physically. Generally speaking someone who breaks into your home while clearly brandishing a gun or a knife is turning himself into a legitimate target. This is just one clear cut scenario.

"What you are actually defending is the right to private property"

Another is when someone is just robbing you without knowing you are home or without becoming a deadly threat. In your state it is extremely unlikely that you can shoot someone in the back as they attempt to retreat from your home with a television set.

Of course it can be argued that the right to kill in defense of your private property is actually the defense not of the television set, but of the principle, essential to civilization, that the television is, after all, your property and not the criminal's. What you are actually defending is the *right* to private property (not a specific piece of property) which seems worth killing for. We have fought wars in defense of this principle throughout the long period of human history (including the imperialism of the axis powers of World War II) during which so-called civilizations believed that conquest was the foremost foundation of economic progress. War is what happens when we stop believing that private property is a human right which no one has the right to violate.

But you will have to engage in a long and intense political project to get your state legislature to recognize that the crime rate would probably be negligible if and when the criminal is faced with the right of the law-abiding individual to defend his property with his life.

Currently, we know of no state which recognizes your right to defend the *principle* of private property with deadly force. Typically the notion is that the television, the jewelry, or the horse for that matter, is not worth the life of the criminal running away with it. Although this would not be convincing to someone in the old west where the theft of his horse might be a death sentence or someone today who is being car-jacked in the desert, it seems to be convincing to most legislators. The bottom line is: While in your home do not shoot someone who is not a physical threat (by virtue of being in retreat) simply because they are robbing you. Just let him get out of your house and call the police. Lock the door behind him.

But what if someone tries to reenter your house to grab still another television? You are warning him not to enter. This time he is not retreating, he is already approaching you in your home or is trying to break in. This time you cannot know that he is not a physical threat. You may be in reasonable fear of great bodily harm or death. Obviously, if he is armed this is an even clearer case of self-defense. (1) He is not retreating but advancing. (2) He is armed. (3) He is breaking into your home or is in your home from which you do not have to retreat. (4) You have warned him. If we take away (2) you still have a case for self-defense.

It can be more frightening to be woken in the middle of the night by the sounds of a break-in, or an even a more subtle intruder, than to be squared off with the criminal at the door, or in some public place, any other time of the day. Above all else, waking up in a fog is much more dangerous to you and your family without a home defense plan which everyone is trained in than it is with one which has been practiced. Not having an alarm system which is screaming in the home invaders ear and convincing him he has just made a big mistake is not good preparation.

"You have to have a plan, the right illumination options, and a weapon that can be wielded effectively around corners."

Having an upstairs is a clear advantage. And cell phones, which have no wires that can be cut, are another tactical advantage for the contemporary home defender.

The first thing that should happen, upstairs or downstairs, is the 911 call to the police. But it will take more time for the police to get there than you can afford if you are serious about defending your family or just your own life. You have to have a plan, the right illumination options, and a weapon that can be wielded effectively around corners.

A first principle is that you must get in between the invader and your children, if any. Ideally, the kids are further down the hallway than the master bedroom. When you emerge from the bedroom you are already in between the invader and the kids.

This intervention is obviously more substantial when you are all upstairs to begin with. If there is just one stairway that an invader can use to get upstairs, you have a bottleneck and you are on the high ground.

Some people, who can afford it, build a 'panic room' inside the house. And people who can afford a panic room usually have homes with a second story. That is where the room is located. A panic room is so well armored that you will want everyone in it during a break-in event. But if you do not have a panic room, it becomes a serious tactical question whether you want the spouse and the kids all concentrated in one room once you start executing your home defense plan. This may make it easier for the criminal to take control of the situation.

"The kids must know what to do ahead of time when you announce an event."

The kids must know what to do ahead of time when you announce an event. You may have them take cover under their beds or in a closet they can lock. You may want them to gather in one room with your spouse where you have a floor which a bullet would have a difficult time penetrating or where they are trained to get behind cover like a queen sized mattress. A bathtub is good cover. But one thing to keep in mind is what gunfire from the first floor can do.

It is perfectly obvious that the chief tactical question associated with any decision to leave the house, especially through some second story exit (which may make it dangerous to reach the ground) is: Is there just as much if not more danger outside than inside the house? What is operational here is that most of the time you will not know. The default decision is to stay inside and defend the family there. This is very much *unlike* dealing with a fire.

Whether you have a second story or not, the second objective, after getting the police on their way, is to get in between the home invader and your family as your family does what it has been trained to do – take cover. Now, what you need is the kind of gun and illumination which makes it

"A gun without a round in the chamber is useless."

easy for you to take cover and eliminate the threat.

Someone alone in, say, an apartment, should simply get down on the side of the bed opposite from the doorway to the bedroom. The gun, retrieved quickly from the safe on the bed stand, or which is already deployed nearby for the night (the better option) can be aimed over the edge of the mattress at the door. The gun should already have a round chambered. Under stressful conditions like a break-in you can easily forget that you have not chambered a round, and this can kill you and/or your family. A gun without a round in the chamber is useless. An indispensable part of your home defense plan is a handgun safe on your bed stand which either opens reliably and quickly when it senses your hand print, or when you enter a code, or which is the secure location of the gun only during the day. At night the gun should be nearby, outside of the safe (though outside your immediate arms' reach if you suffer from sleep disturbances or are otherwise worried about accidentally discharging the weapon in your sleep), with a round in the chamber (if it is a pistol), and otherwise fully loaded, so all you have to do is pick it up and aim. Remembering a combination to a safe under stress is too much of a gamble.

The next step is make sure that you stay calm enough to identify the threat. You must be able to illuminate the criminal, and do so in a blinding way. You must be sure it is not someone whom you do not want to harm. There are many good, affordable flashlights available these days for tactical situations like home defense. There are pistols which you can attach small flash lights to which have a very bright, blinding effect. They are usually attached underneath the barrel of the gun. This is the best option for people who might otherwise have a hard time learning how to wield the flash light in one hand and the gun in the other.

Some experts think that the best home defense gun, especially for a woman, is a twenty-gauge shotgun. It is certainly intimidating in anyone's hands. But consider how easily you can point a handgun around a corner. In fact a short-barreled AR style black rifle may be easier to point around a corner than a shotgun. You should practice at home by actually taking up your planned position and pointing in all relevant directions with both types of guns. This can teach you just how essential handguns are to self-defense. There is a reason why they exist. They increase exponentially our capacity to defend ourselves effectively under every conceivable circumstance.

One of the biggest drawbacks to the shotgun is that it does not hold much ammunition. A break action shotgun is not an option. It holds only two rounds. (It is obviously better than nothing.) A home defense shotgun should hold eight rounds and a minimum of five. This will boost your confidence.

An AR style rifle might back you up with thirty rounds, and a nine millimeter pistol with seventeen. Knowing that you can keep shooting after missing is very important to staying calm and confident.

Some home defense flashlights can be mounted on shotguns and AR 15 style black rifles. The AR 15 is an excellent, highly intimidating home defense weapon. But it cannot be kept in a small safe on your bed stand. But this should not be considered a serious disadvantage. At night, your gun, once again, should be ready to hand and ready to go. You can pick up an AR 15 just as quickly as a handgun.

Both mounted and unmounted flashlights may have a setting which flashes rapidly, intermittently. This is so blinding it will virtual disable an intruder's eye sight.

Once you have identified who has broken in – that he is someone you do not know, or who may be concealed by some kind of mask, or who is obviously carrying some kind of weapon, you have acquired your target. If they are unarmed and far enough away to make hesitation safe, you might warn them. They might withdraw. Otherwise, with an understanding of the applicable laws in your state, you are ready to shoot.

You are executing this plan from a fixed location where you have good cover

"Do not turn on any lights. Do not illuminate yourself. Instead illuminate the criminal in a blinding way. The dark is to your advantage."

yourself. You are not trying to clear the house. Let the police clear the whole house when they get there. Once you have reached your defensive position where you know that you are in between the invader and your family, your only objective is to keep the invader from hurting you or your family behind you, down the hallway. If you start clearing the house by yourself you are putting yourself and your family at unnecessary risk. If you leave your station, the invader may gain access to your family.

Do not turn on any lights. Do not illuminate yourself. Instead illuminate the criminal in a blinding way. If you can afford night vision equipment you can remain concealed in the dark and be able to observe the criminal in your home without him knowing it. This perfects the element of surprise. The dark is to your advantage. You know your home better than the invader.

It is unlikely that your home will be broken into by more than two perps at the same time. Stay in between them and your family. If you take down one of them from your fixed position the other is likely to flee. Also, if you take down one perp do not automatically assume the threat is over, as there may be others of whom you are unaware.

What if they manage to wound or kill you? In that case your family must have a second line of defense. Your spouse should be armed and ready to shoot to kill when a home invader enters the room where she and the kids are taking cover.

What if someone invades your home during the day, when the family is spread out over several rooms?

This should trigger an attempt by everyone to get into the same positions they would take in your night time plan. If this is impossible you should have already identified where to take cover in various places in the house.

But obviously the most important thing is where to keep a gun you can retrieve quickly under this daytime invasion scenario. If you do not keep a gun on your hip until you retire for the night, then you should have some kind of safe or otherwise secure location that you can quickly retrieve a weapon from in both the front and back of the downstairs of your home.

The possibility of a daytime home invasion is what reminds us that both the spouse and the children should be trained to retrieve a gun and use it. Very young children have not only been trained to handle guns safely, they have actually saved their own life and the lives of adults by dispatching home invaders. Obviously you have to carefully assess the ability of your children to deal with such a stressful situation. One thing is clear. Their confidence with guns will dramatically increase their ability to stop someone from victimizing them. The most important training issue is the identification of the threat. They must have it drilled into them that they have to know who they are shooting at, or not shooting at, when the time comes.

Some experts may think that any subadult will be better with the shotgun they have been taught to hunt with. But again, the relatively unwieldy nature of any long gun under extreme circumstances may lead you to train and test your teenaged children with appropriate handguns.

Neither homes nor the families they house, for the purposes of self-defense, are unique. There are a limited number of configurations. Odds are, your situation is not unusual, and professionals in your area who teach people how to defend their homes, day and night, have almost certainly dealt with both a home and a family like your own. They can help you lay out a plan in one home visit, and support your whole family on the safe and effective use of the appropriate weapons. This project will make you and family feel safer, and that alone is worth the cost. If and when the plan and the training actually saves lives, it becomes the wisest investment of a lifetime.

APPENDICES

APPENDIX A

STATE LAW CONCERNING THE TRANSPORT AND CARRY OF FIREARMS

- www.usacarry.com/concealed_carry_permit_information.html
- www.handgunlaw.us/
- www.gunstocarry.com/gun-laws-state/
- www.nraila.org/gun-laws/
- en.wikipedia.org/wiki/Gun_laws_in_the_United_States_by_state
- en.wikipedia.org/wiki/Concealed_carry_in_the_United_States
- itunes.apple.com/us/app/ccw-concealed-carry-50-state-guide/id443321291

  The last link is for a phone app which makes the information mobile.